Y0-CDF-475

UNIT 4 Patterns in the Sky

Stories of SPACE

The McGraw-Hill Companies

www.WrightGroup.com

Copyright © 2011 by The McGraw-Hill Companies, Inc.

All rights reserved. Except as permitted under the United States Copyright Act, no part of this publication may be reproduced or distributed in any form or by any means, or stored in a database or retrieval system, without the prior written permission from the publisher, unless otherwise indicated.

Printed in USA.

Send all inquiries to:
Wright Group/McGraw-Hill
P.O. Box 812960
Chicago, IL 60681

ISBN 978-0-07-656409-5
MHID 0-07-656409-6

4 5 6 7 8 9 DOC 16 15 14 13 12 11

Contents

Digital 21

My Home Page

ebook

online coach

Why do people study space?

Have you ever looked into the night sky and wondered about it? What are the stars made of? Where did they come from? Over the centuries, people have come up with many ideas about the night sky. Some of these ideas are being changed as scientists learn more.

Focus Questions

What patterns and cycles do we find in space?

Selection 2

How did people of the past explain objects in the night sky?

Selection 3

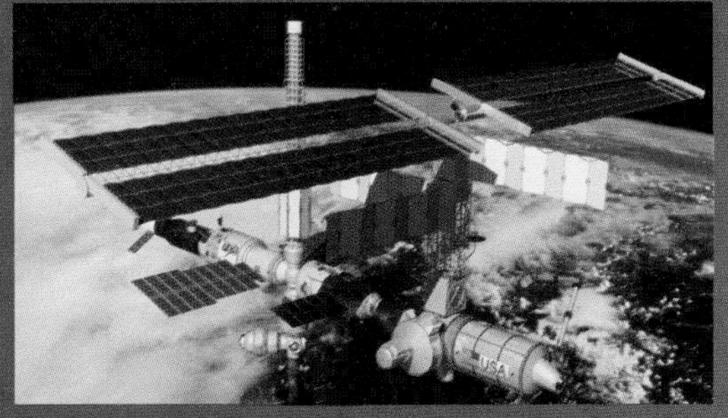

How do people view space today?

Selection 4

How might space be a part of our future?

Preview 

What patterns and cycles do we find in space? Preview pages 6–27. Then read *Edwin Hubble: Star Explorer* to find out.

Selection 1

Edwin Hubble: STAR EXPLORER

BY MEISH GOLDISH

CHAPTER ONE Science Student

Edwin Hubble began to love science when he was only a child. At age eight, he looked through a **telescope** for the first time. He saw hundreds of stars **sparkling** in the distant sky—only they appeared much larger and closer in the telescope.

Hubble's grandfather explained that stars are giant suns that give off light and heat. They are trillions of miles from Earth.

distant: faraway

This type of eclipse happens only when there is a full moon.

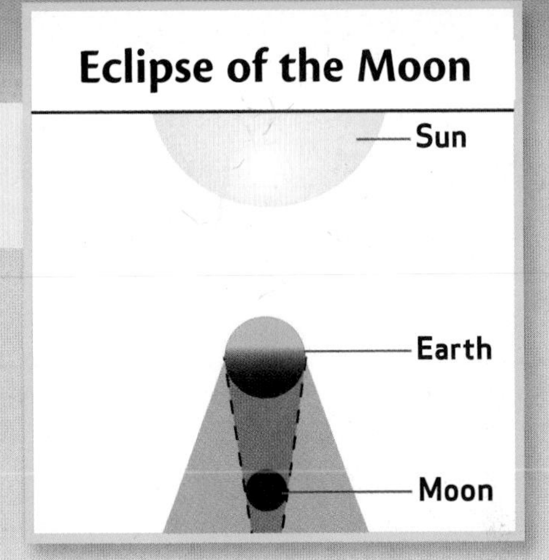

Young Hubble was fascinated with astronomy—the study of the stars, planets, and space. He was excited to see an eclipse of the moon in 1899.

In an eclipse of the moon, the sun, Earth, and the moon line up so that Earth blocks the sunlight that **reflects** off the moon. Earth's shadow shades the moon, making it darker and darker until it cannot be seen.

Hubble's interest in science grew as he got older. In college he studied mathematics and astronomy.

Edwin Hubble

Hubble's father wanted his son to become a lawyer. In 1913 Hubble set up a law office in Kentucky, but he was not happy in his career. He tried teaching instead.

After teaching high school for a year, Hubble returned to college for higher studies. To earn money, he worked at the school's Yerkes Observatory in Chicago, Illinois. It had one of the world's largest telescopes at the time. It was 60 feet long!

Many scientists worked at the Yerkes Observatory. Hubble is seen here in the back row, fifth from the right.

Hubble worked with the giant telescope. He used it to take a picture of fuzzy clouds of light in the sky called **nebulae**.

Scientists did not agree about the location of the nebulae. Some thought they were in our **galaxy**, the Milky Way. Other scientists believed they were farther away. Hubble was not sure who was right, but he wanted to find out.

Nebulae are clouds of gas and dust that are found between stars.

CHAPTER TWO A Major Discovery

After finishing school Hubble fought overseas in World War I. When he returned he worked at the Mount Wilson Observatory in California. It had a telescope even more powerful than the one at Yerkes.

Hubble wished to settle the question of the location of the nebulae. Were they part of Earth's galaxy, or were they outside our galaxy? To find out, Hubble first had to figure out how far away the nebulae were.

overseas: across the ocean

The Hooker Telescope

Hubble worked with the Hooker Telescope at the Mount Wilson Observatory. At the time, it was the most powerful telescope on Earth. Its mirror, which makes items look larger, was 100 inches (2.54 meters) wide.

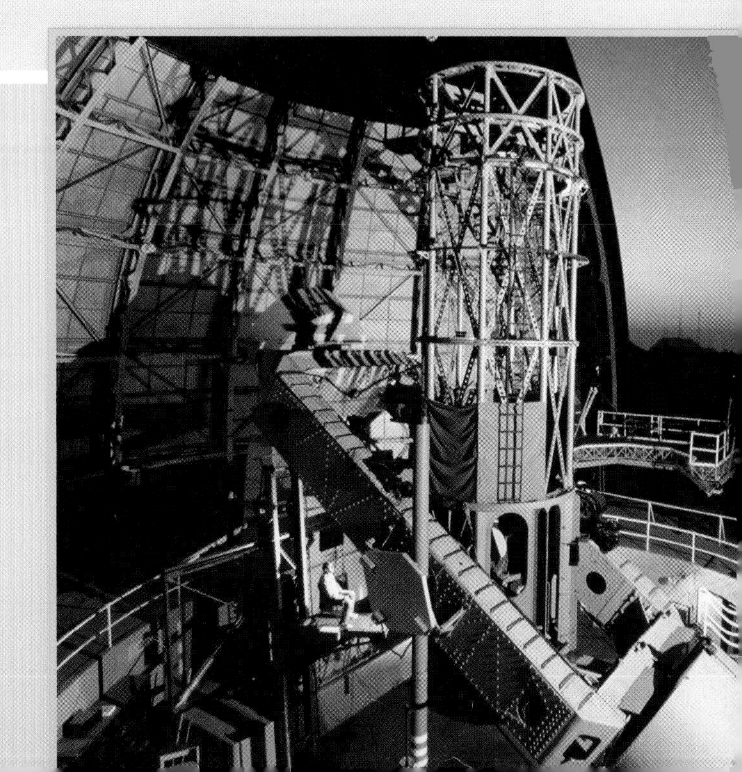

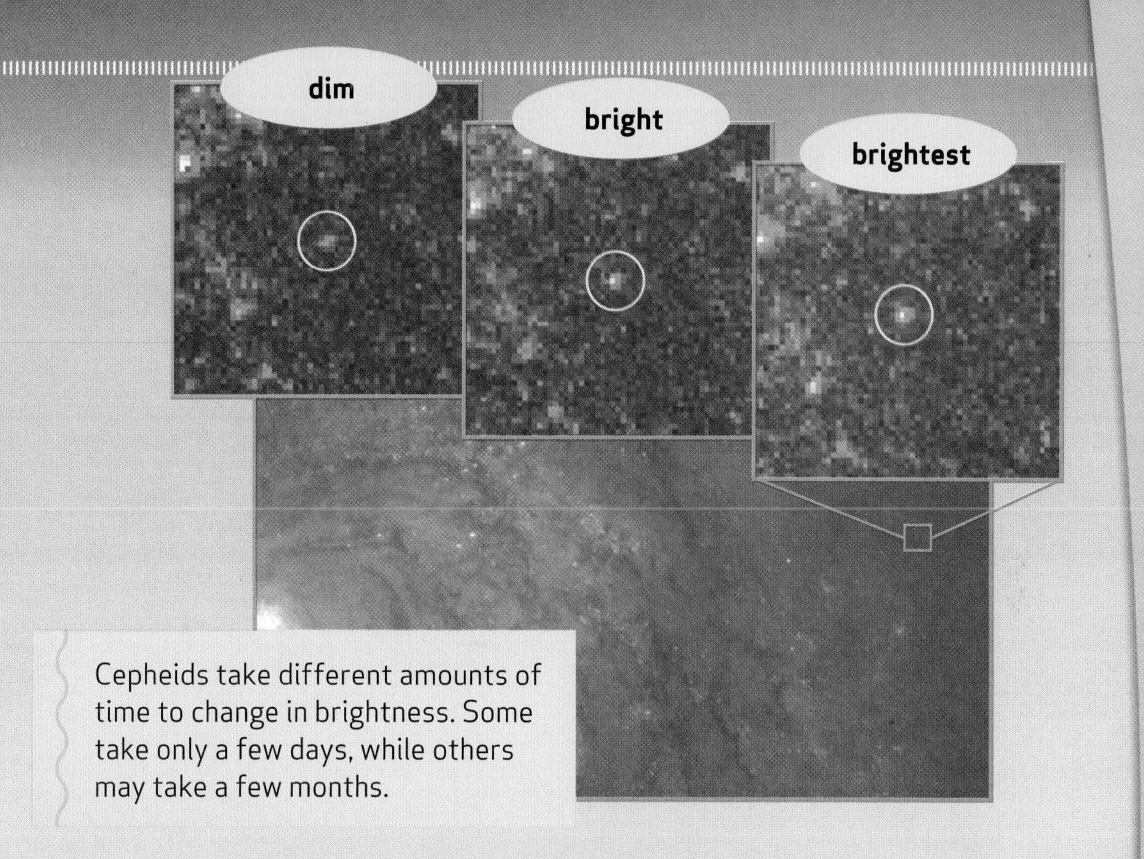

Cepheids take different amounts of time to change in brightness. Some take only a few days, while others may take a few months.

Hubble took pictures of stars called Cepheids. These stars grow brighter and dimmer over time. Hubble measured their brightness. He also measured how long it took for each Cepheid to grow dim.

With this information Hubble was able to determine how far the nebulae were from Earth. His measurements led him to the answer. The nebulae he saw were too far away to be part of our galaxy.

determine: figure out

Hubble shared his discoveries about nebulae. He wrote a paper that explained his findings. The paper stated that there are nebulae outside the Milky Way. He also learned that some of these nebulae weren't nebulae at all. They were other galaxies! Hubble's work led astronomers to realize that there are many galaxies in the universe.

Hubble's discovery was as important as the discoveries that Earth **rotates** and that it **revolves** around the sun. Hubble's ideas changed how scientists saw the sky.

Today scientists know of millions of galaxies, not just one.

Strategy Tool Kit
Make Connections
Name another important discovery in science. How is it important?

Hubble's wife, Grace, kept journals of the important events in their lives.

CHAPTER THREE A New Law

In 1924 Hubble married Grace Leib. She greatly admired her husband and his work.

Hubble kept on studying galaxies in space. He discovered many other galaxies. He used a powerful telescope to study their shapes. Now Hubble wanted to find a way to **classify** all the different galaxies he was studying.

Over time Hubble found a way to classify the galaxies. He sorted them by distance, shape, and brightness. His system became known as the Hubble Sequence.

Look at the bar graph below. It classifies the 160 largest galaxies in a group called the Virgo Cluster. It sorts them based on their shape. Some galaxies look like regular spirals (S). Some galaxies look like ellipses and are called elliptical galaxies (E). Some spiral galaxies have a bar in the center (SB). Some galaxies look **irregular** (I).

spiral galaxy

system: way of organizing

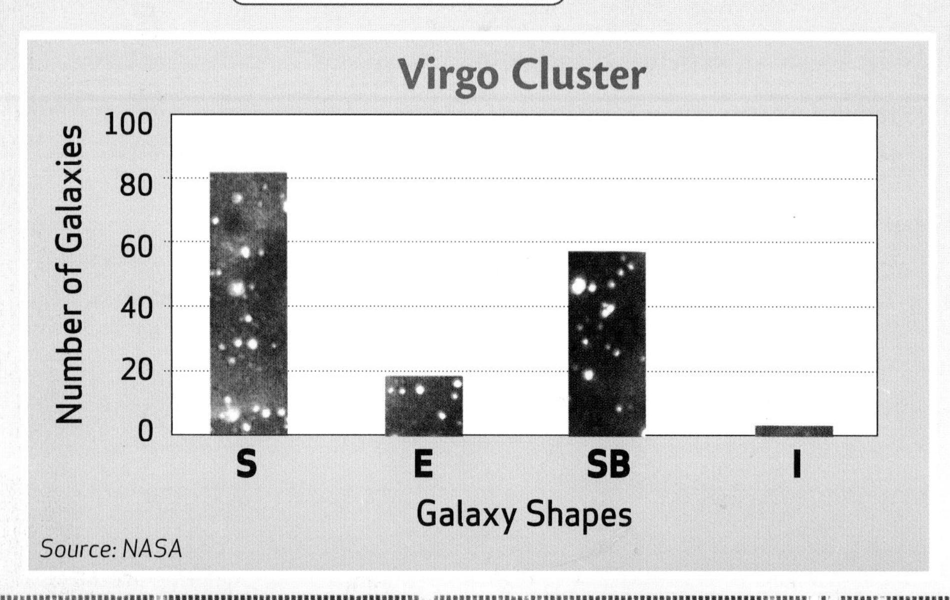

Next Hubble took on a new **puzzle**. For years the light from the galaxies he observed had looked strange. At times the light seemed redder than it should be. Hubble believed the change had to do with how far each galaxy was from Earth.

Hubble observed many galaxies carefully and saw that they were moving away from each other. He measured the distances from Earth to these galaxies. There was a connection between these distances and how quickly the galaxies were moving.

observed: watched

With his discoveries, Hubble formed a new rule. It was called Hubble's Law. The law said that the farther apart two galaxies are, the faster they move away from each other.

Hubble's Law proved that the **universe** was expanding. Scientists once thought the universe never changed in size. Instead Hubble showed that the universe is like a balloon that keeps getting bigger and bigger.

expanding: growing bigger

Hubble came up with his new law about galaxies in 1929.

In 1931 Einstein (3rd from right) visited Hubble (2nd from left) to congratulate him in person.

Hubble's Law amazed many scientists. One of them was Albert Einstein, the most famous scientist of the century. Twelve years earlier, Einstein had the idea that the universe was changing, either growing or getting smaller. However, other scientists told him he was wrong about a changing universe.

Finally Einstein agreed that his idea must be wrong. Hubble's discovery made him very happy. It showed Einstein that his earlier idea had been correct after all.

The Big Bang Theory

Hubble's Law supports another idea about the universe called the Big Bang theory. A Belgian scientist named Georges Lemaitre and a Russian scientist named Alexander Friedmann had come up with this idea several years earlier.

Lemaitre and Friedmann believed that the universe was one small speck about 10 billion years ago. Then a huge flash or bang caused the universe to start expanding. Not all scientists agree that the Big Bang theory is correct.

speck: tiny bit

The Big Bang theory says the universe is expanding.

Stop and Think
Why was Edwin Hubble's work important to other scientists?

CHAPTER FOUR Sharing with Others

Hubble **desired** to share his discoveries with people who were not scientists. In 1936 he wrote a book called *The Realm of the Nebulae*. It sold many copies.

Hubble was invited to speak at several colleges. He went across the United States and England, giving lectures at schools.

lectures: speeches

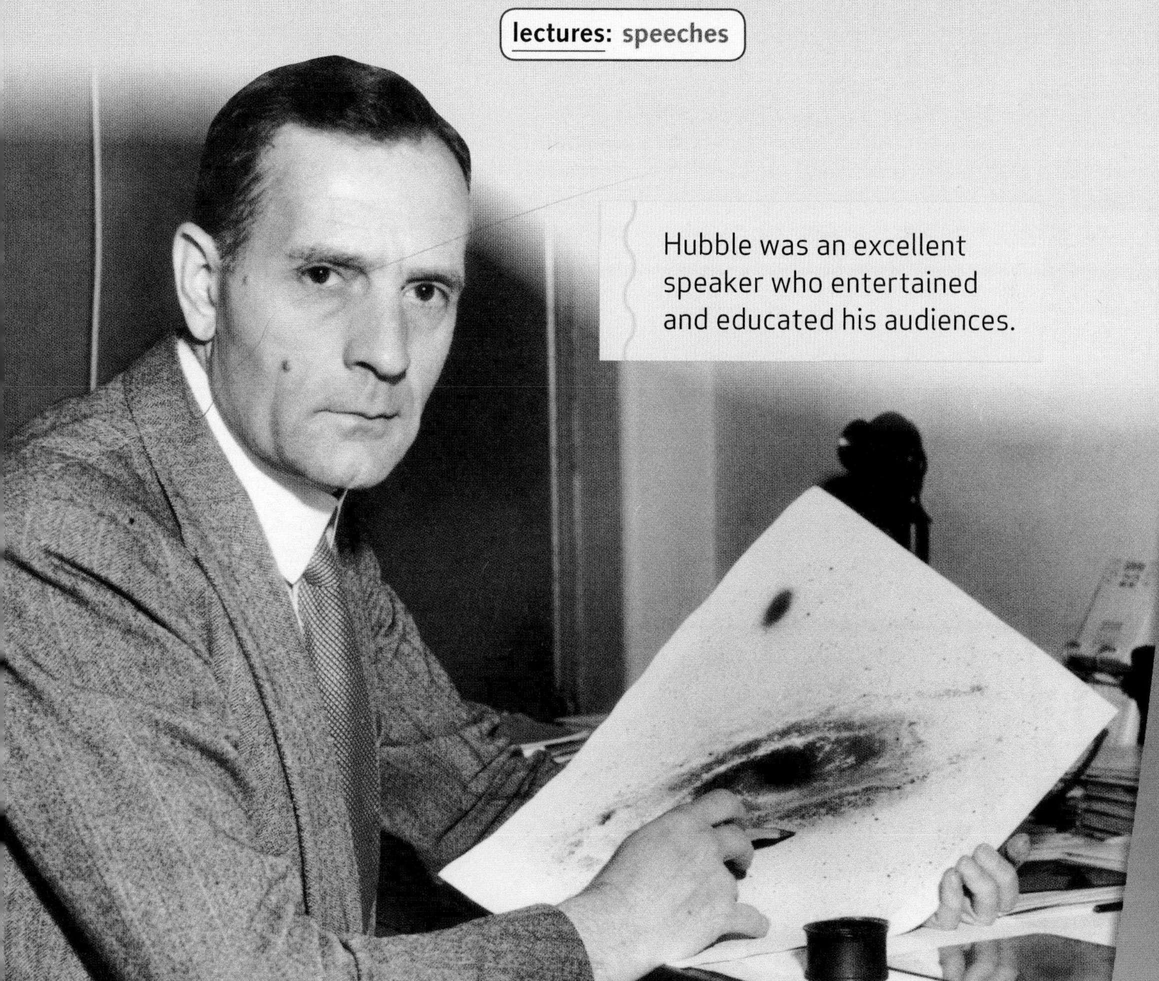

Hubble was an excellent speaker who entertained and educated his audiences.

Many people wanted to meet Hubble—even Hollywood stars. He received many visitors at the Mount Wilson Observatory.

There was still work to do at the observatory. Hubble wanted to discover more objects even farther away in space. For that he would need a more powerful telescope.

Hubble began to design the largest telescope on Earth. It was called the Hale Telescope. It would be four times as powerful as the Hooker Telescope.

design: plan

Visitors can tour the Mount Wilson Observatory and attend lectures.

The new telescope was to be placed at another observatory in California. However, building it took many years. Work had to be stopped during World War II, when Hubble left his job to serve his country.

At first Hubble wanted to fight in the army, as he had done in World War I. Yet he soon realized he could help more as a scientist than as a soldier.

realized: discovered

Hubble was put in charge of ballistics at an army base in Maryland. Ballistics is the study of how bullets, bombs, and rockets fly through the air. At the army base, Hubble tested new weapons. He made new designs to improve the way they moved. However, Hubble saw how atomic bombs destroyed life in Japan. Later he spoke out against their use.

Hubble received a special award from the U.S. government for his help during World War II.

CHAPTER FIVE Sad News

After World War II ended in 1945, Hubble returned to his job. The Hale Telescope was finally finished in 1948. The entire telescope weighed 500 tons. That's as heavy as a large ship!

With the new telescope Hubble hoped to answer some new questions. How big is the universe? Is there an end point in space? How many nebulae and galaxies are out there?

The Hale Telescope was the largest telescope until 1993. It is still used today.

Hubble was honored by being the first person to use the new Hale Telescope. A reporter asked him what he hoped to find with it. Hubble answered, "We hope to find something we hadn't expected."

Indeed, something unexpected did happen, but it was not what anyone had hoped for. In 1949 Hubble had a major heart attack. No one was sure at first if he would live or not.

unexpected: surprising

This is the first photograph taken by Hubble with the Hale Telescope in 1949.

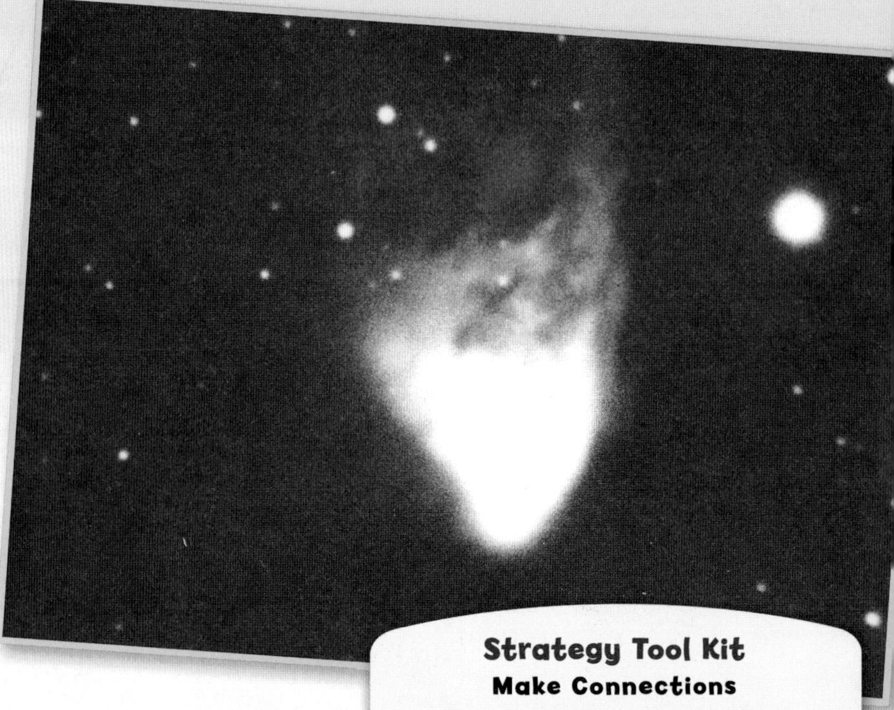

Strategy Tool Kit
Make Connections
What would you hope to find if you were studying space with a powerful telescope?

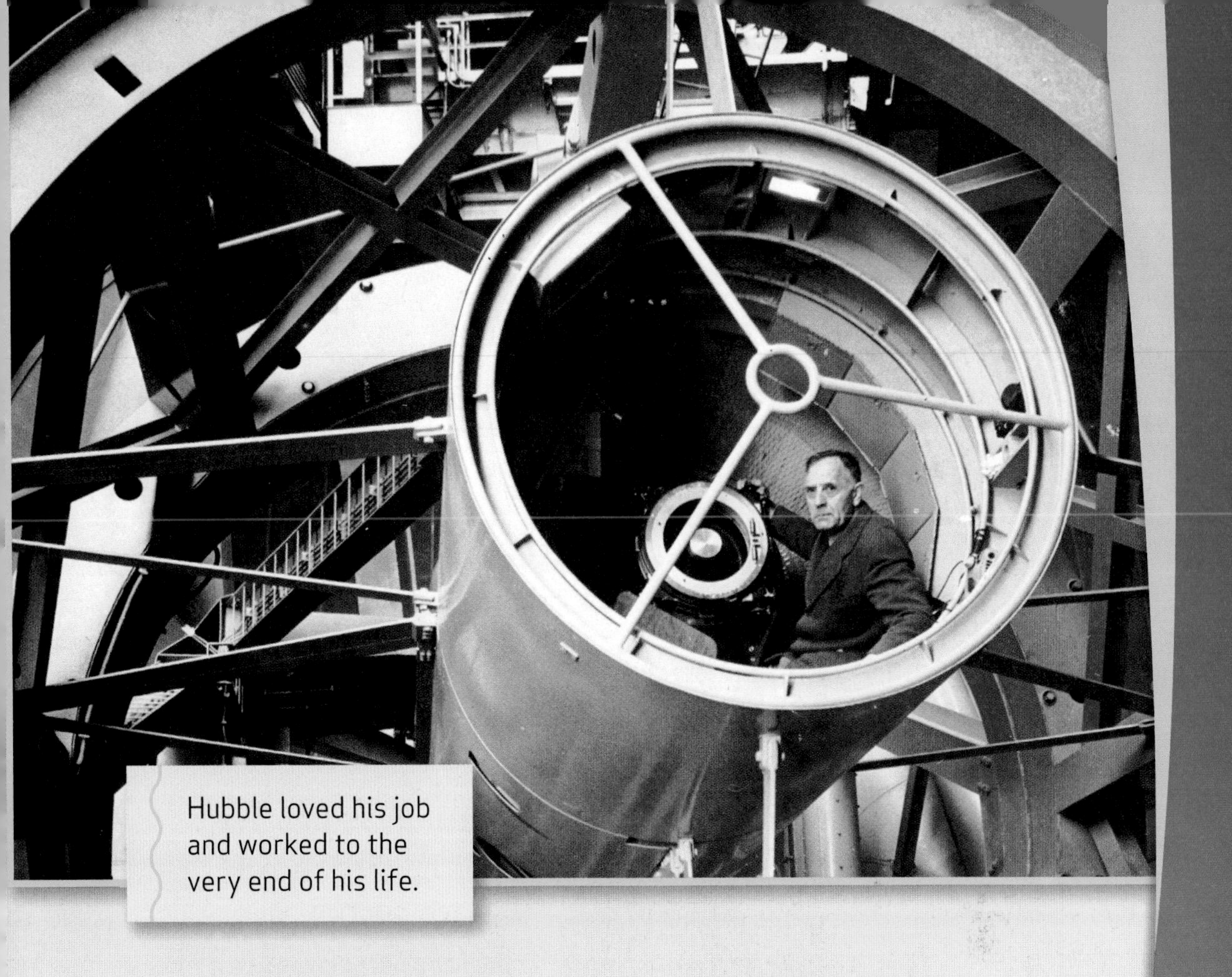

Hubble loved his job and worked to the very end of his life.

Hubble did live, but he was now much weaker. Four months after his heart attack, he slowly began to return to work. However, he could not stay in the observatory in the winter. The air was much too cold. Working at a slower pace, Hubble explored new galaxies as best he could.

In 1953 at the age of sixty-three, Hubble died of a heart attack. The world had lost a great scientist.

This astronaut is repairing the Hubble Telescope.

Hubble received many awards during his life. Yet one of his greatest honors came after he died. A new space telescope was sent into the sky in 1990. It was named the Hubble Telescope.

The telescope is as big as a school bus. It was designed to move through space taking pictures of nebulae, galaxies, and planets, including Earth. The Hubble Telescope changed the way astronomers view space, just as Hubble himself did.

Strategy Tool Kit
Summarize
What are some of Hubble's accomplishments?

Sum It Up

Hubble changed the world with his work. He proved that the universe has not just one galaxy, but millions of them. He found a way to classify the galaxies. He came up with Hubble's Law, proving that the universe is expanding. He helped to design and build the world's biggest telescope.

Hubble was a great man who helped us to see the universe in a whole new way. His achievements will never be forgotten.

achievements: successes

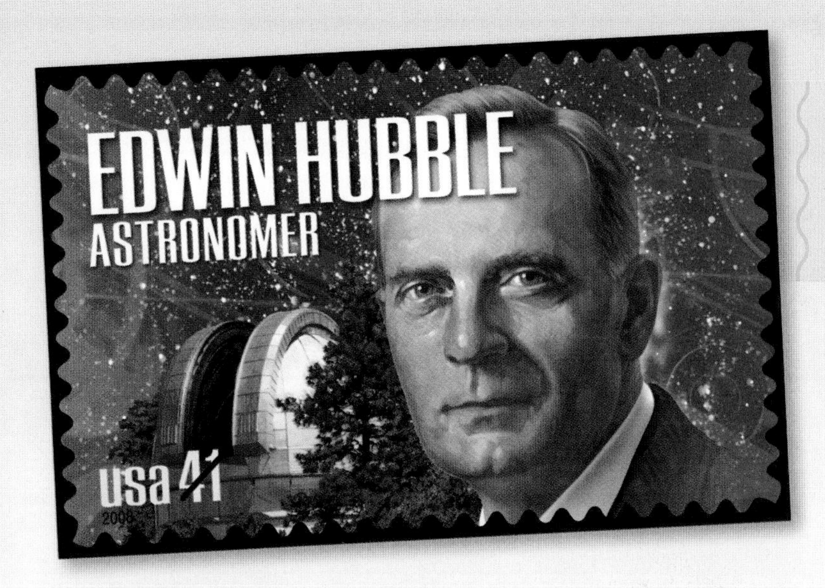

In 2008 the U.S. Post Office introduced a new stamp in honor of Hubble.

Focus Question: What patterns and cycles do we find in space?

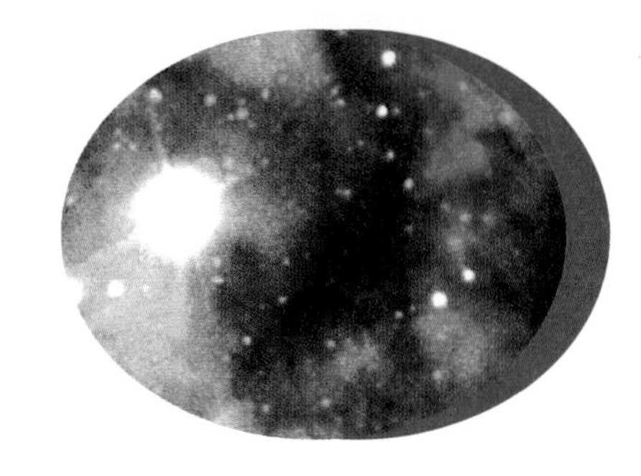

A Check Understanding ★

Make a list of the patterns and cycles Edwin Hubble found while studying space. PRACTICE COMPANION 293

B Understand Text Features ★★

Look at the bar graph on page 14. Show the bar graph to a partner. Explain what information in the text the graph helps you understand.

C Share and Compare ★★

Compare your list of patterns and cycles with a partner's list. Are any of the patterns and cycles the same? Are any different? Explain why.

D Think Critically ★★★★

Why do people study space? Use examples from the selection to explain.

Think Ahead
Selection 2

Focus Question: How did people of the past explain objects in the night sky?

Selection Connection

You have learned about the kinds of discoveries scientists have made about patterns and cycles in space. In the next selection you will learn why people study space.

Show What You Know

Think about the following: *the moon*, *the stars*, and *the sky at night*. Do you know any stories about these things? Write your ideas. PRACTICE COMPANION **294**

Preview

How did people of the past explain objects in the night sky? Preview pages 30–53. Then read *Here Comes the Sun!* to find out.

Selection 2

Here Comes the SUN!

by Karen Baicker

CHAPTER 1

Ancient People View the Sun

Long ago, people watched the sun move across the sky. The bright orange ball rose in the morning in the east. It set in the evening in the west. It was easy for people to believe that Earth stood still and that the sun moved over it.

People watched the sun in awe. It affected their lives every day. When the sun came, it brought daylight and heat. It allowed people to grow food. Its warmth and light were necessary to live. When the sun left, all was night and darkness.

People now know that Earth revolves around the sun—not the other way around. But it is still easy to understand why people long ago made up stories about the powerful glowing ball in the sky.

awe: wonder

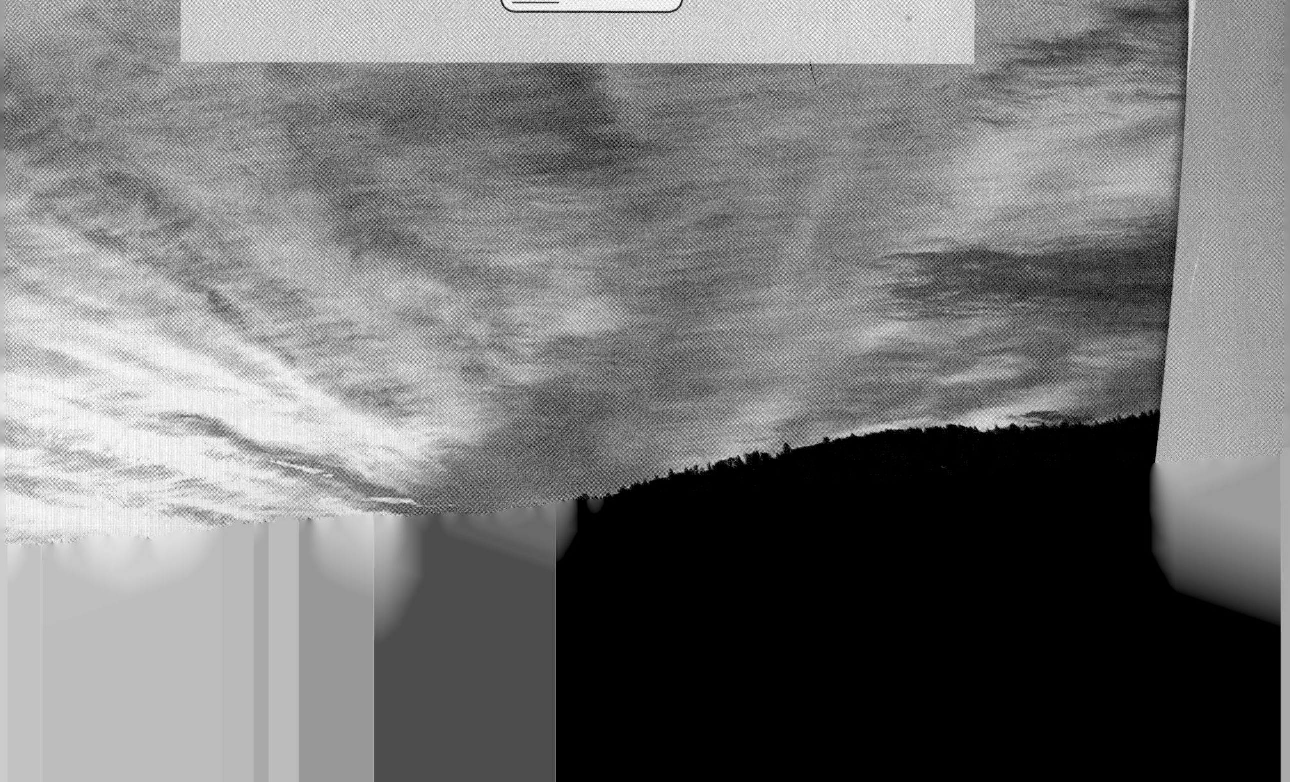

Ra, the Egyptian Sun God

Many ancient people believed the sun was a god. After all, without the sun, there would be no life at all! Ancient Egyptians called their sun god Ra. They thought that Ra made light and all other things. They believed Ra created the first people from his own tears. Those people became parents and gave birth to Earth and the sky.

created: made

In one myth, Ra had a daughter named Hathor. She was considered the goddess of the sky.

Drawings of Ra show a man's body with the head of a hawk. Ra also has a sun disk above his head. Ra is sometimes **portrayed** rowing across the sky in two boats. He uses one boat to travel from day to night and another to sail from night to day.

Helios, the Greek Sun God

The Greeks spoke of a different sun god, named Helios. Helios drove across the sky from east to west in a golden chariot. Then, after sunset, he sailed back and waited for the day to begin again.

The Greek sun god, Helios, had horses pull his chariot across the sky.

The Ten Chinese Suns

The Chinese have a different myth about the sun. Their myth tells of weeks with ten days, instead of seven. For each day of the week, there was a different sun. Every night their mother, Xi, would wash each sun in a lake. She would hang each sun in a large tree to dry. In the morning, one of the ten suns would **depart** for a mountain in the west.

This work of art illustrates the Chinese myth of the ten suns.

The suns became tired of taking these long, lonely trips. One day all ten suns decided to go to the mountain at the same time. Together their heat was too strong, and the earth grew much too hot. Their father sent someone to frighten them so they would move apart. But the person he sent shot nine of the suns with arrows. Their father was very angry. Only one sun was left to **emerge** each day in the sky.

Strategy Tool Kit
Make Connections
How do these myths reflect the ideas people around the world had about the sun?

People have always made up stories to explain the sun. In some stories the sun is a life-giving power. In others the sun is something dangerous to be feared. In many of the stories, the sun is strong and its movement marks time. The sun tells people when one day ends and the next day begins.

Scientists of the Past

Scientists have been studying the sun for hundreds of years. They have used special tools to watch how it changes. These tools have helped scientists collect facts. As a result, today we know much more about the sun and its power.

Early scientists did not have such advanced instruments as this solar telescope.

The sun is very bright. It is too risky to look directly at the sun. Even on a cloudy day, the sun can hurt your eyes if you stare at it. Early scientists realized the danger. They came up with a good way to look at the sun indirectly.

Scientists made boxes called camera obscuras. They aimed light from the sun through a tiny hole in the box. The light passed through the hole and made a picture of the sun on the opposite surface. Scientists could look at the picture and safely study the sun and solar eclipses.

aimed: pointed

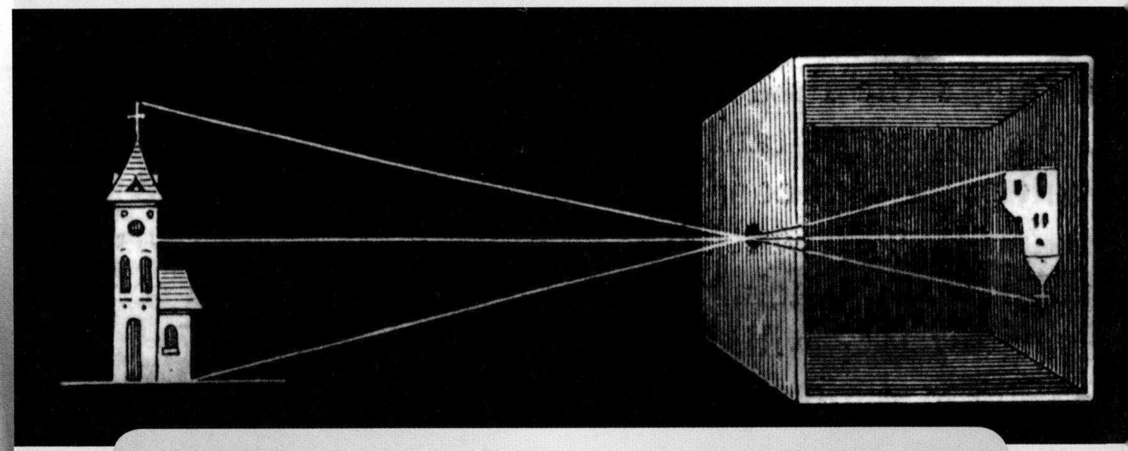

The image projected in a simple camera obscura is upside down because light rays cross when they pass through a very small hole.

What Is a Solar Eclipse?

Clouds sometimes block the sun from view, but even on a clear day, light from the sun can be blocked from above. This is known as a solar eclipse.

During a solar eclipse the moon moves between Earth and the sun. The moon blocks the sun, and the moon takes on a soft halo, or ring of light, around its edges. The sky becomes darker, the brightest stars can be seen, and the temperature becomes cooler.

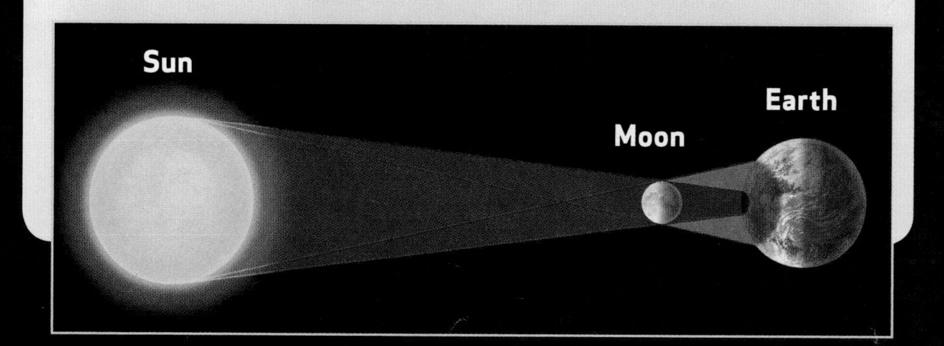

When telescopes were invented in the 1600s, it was still hard to study the sun. Looking at the sun through a telescope was even riskier for people's sight. Astronomers needed to find ways to study the sun without hurting their eyes.

In 1610 the Italian scientist Galileo used the idea of the camera obscura to study the sun. He pointed his telescope at the sun. But he did not look through it. Instead he put a screen behind the telescope's eyepiece. A picture of the sun was **projected** onto the screen.

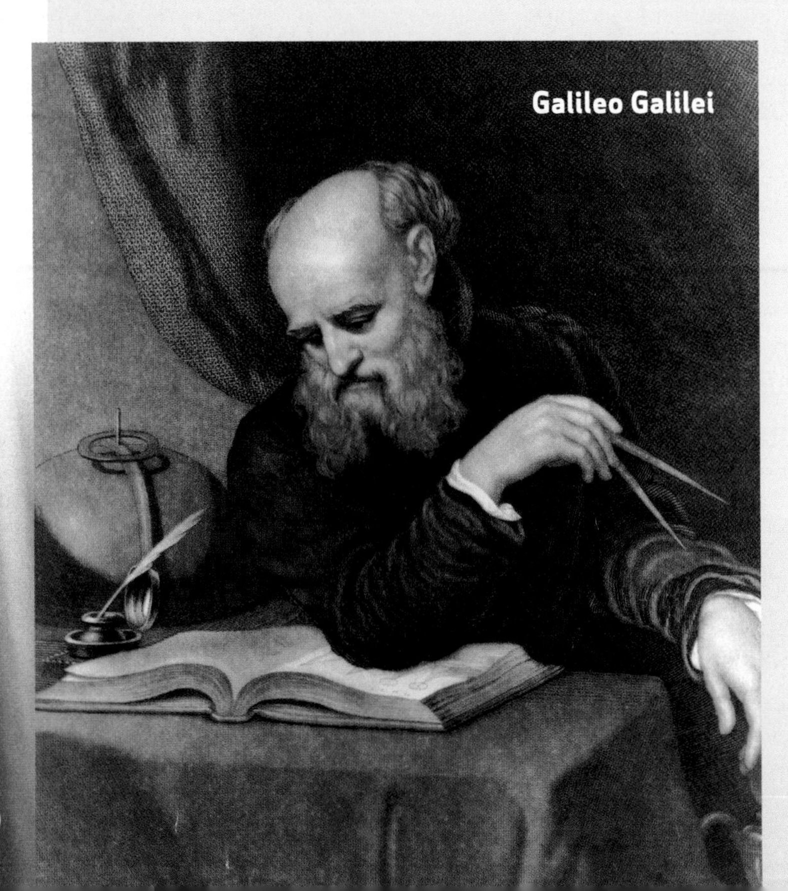
Galileo Galilei

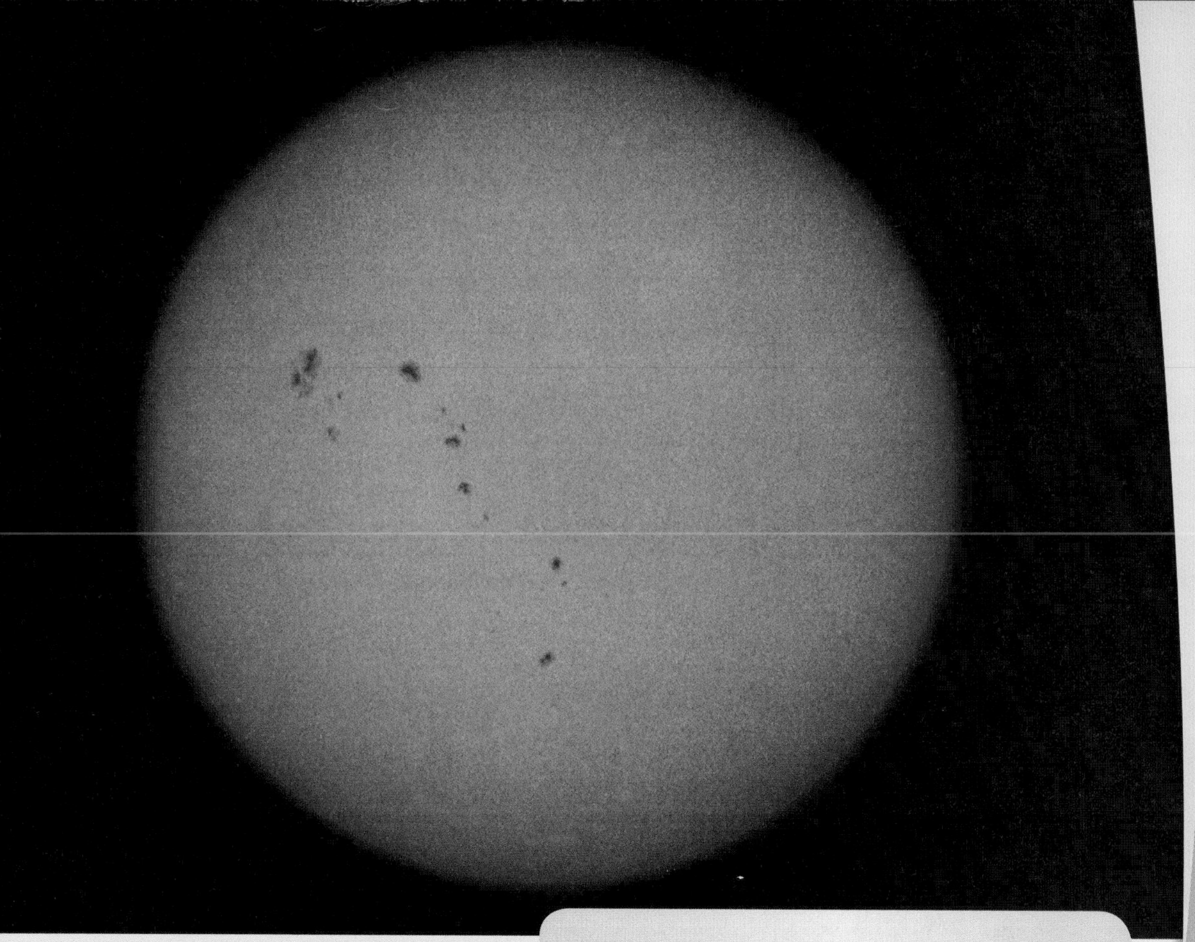

Although sunspots are cooler than the rest of the sun, they're still about 6,000°F.

Sunspots

Some places on the sun are cooler than other places. These places look like dark spots. Galileo noticed such spots on the sun. The sunspots moved and changed shape over time. They helped scientists understand that the sun changes.

noticed: saw

Strategy Tool Kit
Visualize
Picture how Galileo used the idea of the camera obscura to view the sun with his telescope.

By studying sunspots, early scientists hoped to learn what was happening deep inside the sun. They also began to figure out ways to study the sun's light. In the 1600s Isaac Newton used a glass **prism** to break the sun's rays into different colors. These different colors are called the sun's spectrum. The best example of a **visible** spectrum is a rainbow. Other scientists began to study the range of colors and the different light waves traveling from the sun.

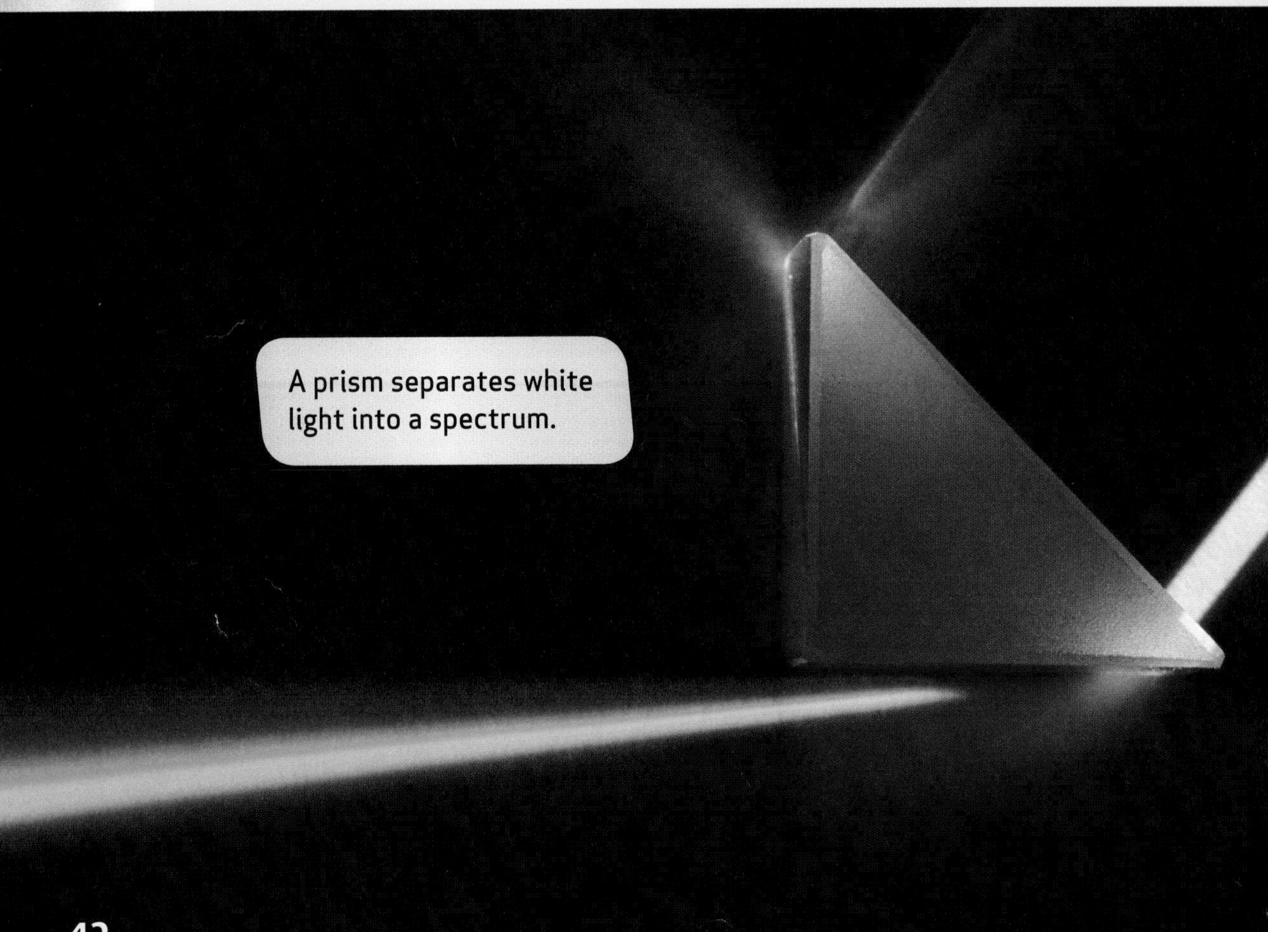

A prism separates white light into a spectrum.

A spectograph, like the one in this photo, splits light so that scientists can study it.

By studying the sun's light waves, scientists found that there were hundreds of tiny dark lines in the sun's spectrum. These dark lines helped scientists figure out what elements were in the sun's atmosphere. Scientists were also able to figure out that the sun is very, very hot.

Solar Flares

In the 1800s scientists began observing solar **flares**. Solar flares happen when **magnetic** energy suddenly escapes from the surface of the sun. They look like bright flashes of light erupting on the surface. Solar flares are very hot. They also let go of very large amounts of energy. In fact the energy released from a solar flare is 10 million times greater than the energy released from an exploding volcano!

Solar flares release large amounts of radiation, a form of energy.

Stop and Think

How did early scientists study the sun? What did they learn?

Solar Learning

As scientists continue to study the sun, their knowledge grows. They now know that the sun, a ball of glowing gases, is a medium-sized star. It looks larger and brighter than other stars because it is the star nearest Earth. Even so, it is 93 million miles away! That's nearly 400 times farther than the distance of the moon from Earth.

Light from the sun travels at a speed of over 186,000 miles per second. At that speed, it still takes about eight minutes to reach Earth.

The sun is much bigger than Earth. It is almost 870,000 miles across. Imagine if the sun were hollow. It would take more than one million Earths to fill it!

Uranus

Neptune

The sun is the center of our solar system. Earth and seven other planets orbit the sun. The planets farthest from the sun receive the least heat and light.

Inside the Sun

Scientists have taken pictures of the way the light shifts, or changes, on the sun. They figured out that the sun **pulses** in and out. From this discovery, scientists began learning more about the inside of the sun.

Scientists now know that the sun has different layers, or regions. The gases near the sun's core, or center, are denser than those near the surface.

The surface of the sun has a temperature of about 10,000 degrees Fahrenheit. Deep inside it's even hotter. At its core the sun is about 27 million degrees Fahrenheit!

The sun's heat comes from a nuclear reaction. Inside the sun, hydrogen atoms are constantly combining to make helium atoms. This process releases energy in the form of heat and light.

Solar Research Today

In 2006 scientists undertook an international mission to study the sun. They launched a specially designed spacecraft from Kyushu, Japan. It was called Hinode (hih-NOH-day). Hinode carries two telescopes and a third instrument to measure speed and temperature. Pictures from the telescopes show details never seen before. Scientists study these details to learn more about the sun's layers and the release of magnetic energy. Data sent to Earth from Hinode is helping scientists better understand sunspots and solar flares.

Looking to the Future

Like all stars, the sun is slowly dying. The bigger the star, the shorter its life will be. The sun is a medium-sized star, but it is big enough to give off the energy needed for life on Earth. And it is not so big that it will die soon. Scientists think the sun will be around for another 10 billion years!

Hinode's orbit was carefully set to keep it in constant sunlight for nine months of the year.

Solar Energy

People are learning to use the power of the sun as energy. Through solar technology, people can make and store heat and electricity. And the sun makes new energy all the time, so it will not be used up.

Using the sun's power is good for Earth. Solar energy is clean. It does not cause air or water pollution. That's one reason scientists are working to develop solar-powered cars and other machines.

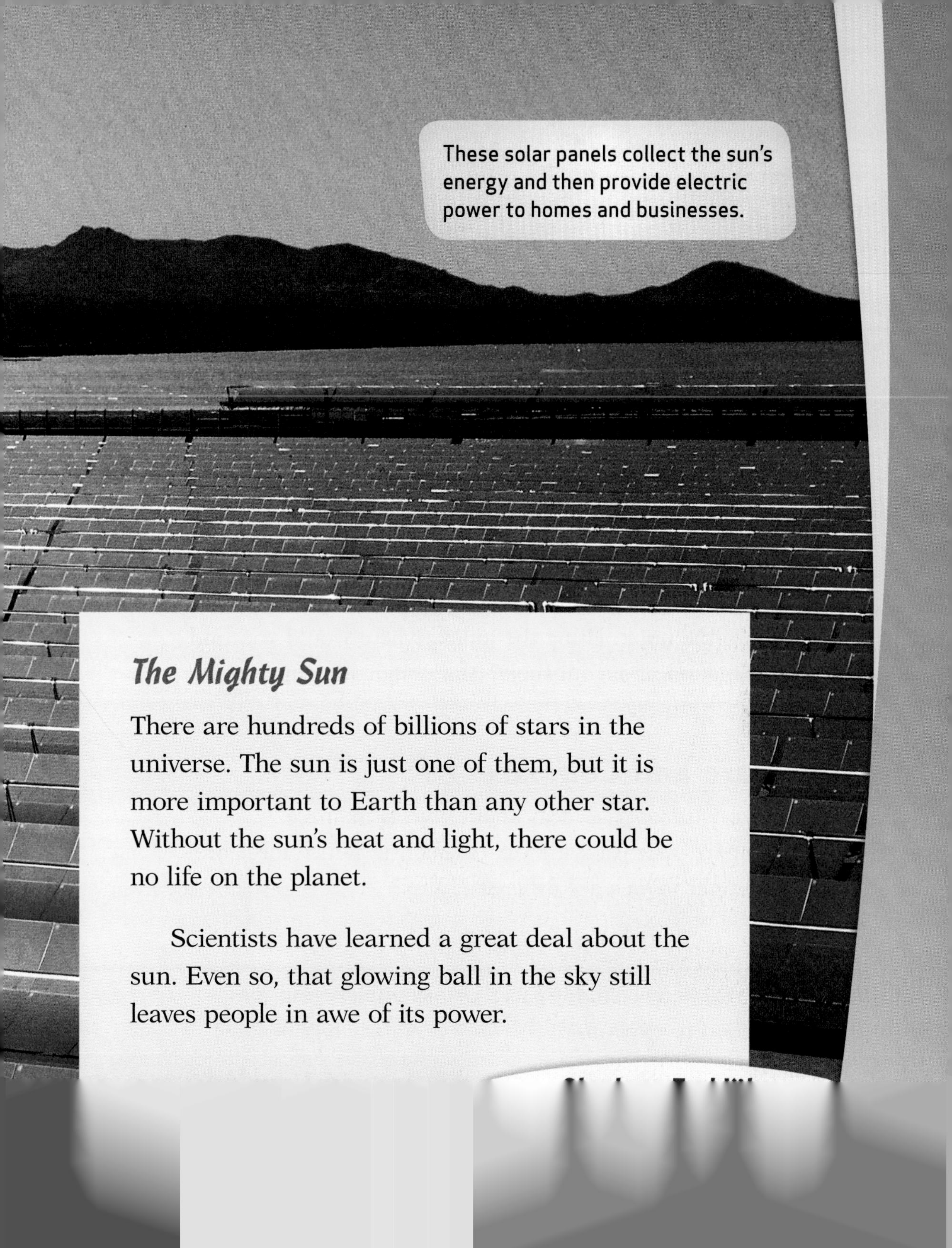

These solar panels collect the sun's energy and then provide electric power to homes and businesses.

The Mighty Sun

There are hundreds of billions of stars in the universe. The sun is just one of them, but it is more important to Earth than any other star. Without the sun's heat and light, there could be no life on the planet.

Scientists have learned a great deal about the sun. Even so, that glowing ball in the sky still leaves people in awe of its power.

Focus Question: How did people of the past explain objects in the night sky?

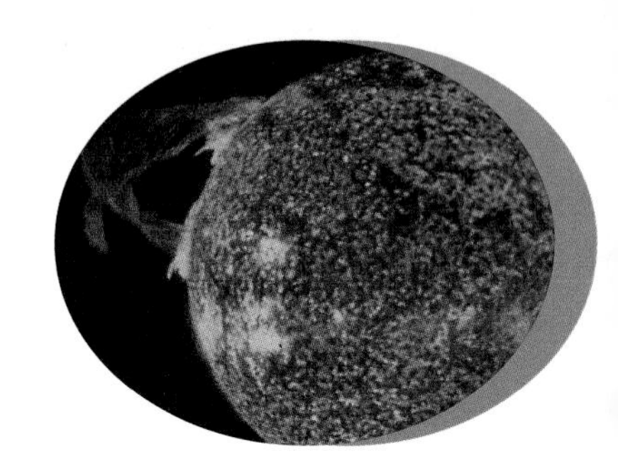

A Check Understanding

How did people of the past explain the sun in the sky? How do their ideas differ from what we know now?

PRACTICE COMPANION 310

B Understand Text Features

An index is an alphabetical list of subjects found at the back of a book. Page numbers help you find the subjects within the book. Using the index, where would you find information about sunspots? Share your information with a partner.

C Share and Compare

Make a list of past ideas about objects in space. Compare your list with a partner's list. Which ideas are the same? Which are different? Why?

D Think Critically

Why do people study space? Use examples from the selection to explain.

Think Ahead
Selection 3

Focus Question: How do people view space today?

Selection Connection

You have learned how people of the past were inspired by the sky. In the next selection you will learn why people study space.

Show What You Know

Think about the following: *telescopes*, *satellites*, and *space vehicles*. How do these things help us view space? Write your ideas.

PRACTICE COMPANION 311

Preview

How do people view space today?
Preview pages 56–77. Then read *Spaceman* to find out.

Spaceman

by Dina McClellan

Illustrated by Janice Fried

Chapter 1 Superman

"Grandpa, I have a question," said Zoe from her end of the porch swing.

"Ask away," said Grandpa.

It was after dinner, and her grandfather had invited her to sit outside "to take in the night," as he liked to put it. Zoe pictured the night as some sort of show, which it kind of was when you watched it with Grandpa.

"When you were a little boy, what did you want to be when you grew up? I mean," said Zoe, "did you always want to be an astronaut?"

"Not really," said Grandpa. "I wanted to be Superman. I *still* want to be Superman."

"Oh, *Grandpa*!" Zoe said. But she loved it when he got silly.

"Well, I can tell you one thing," Grandpa said. "I did *not* think I was going to let myself be strapped into a tiny capsule that was shot into space. And then spend the next three days orbiting Earth! No, sir!"

"I got interested in space when my parents gave me a real, working telescope for my seventh birthday. My dad helped me set it up in the living room in front of this big picture window we had. You could see one **magnificent** sky that went on and on forever. I loved spending time alone with my dad too, learning the names of star **formations**.

"But I have to say that the whole country had gone space-crazy by then.

"That was in the 1950s," Grandpa went on, "and the world had been through a very bad war. We needed to believe that we were headed for a brighter future. So we looked to the sky and decided that the next step was to **conquer** space.

"Another country, the Soviet Union, had the same idea. For many years the two countries took part in what we call the 'space race.' Each country wanted to be the first one to send a man into space."

Strategy Tool Kit

Ask and Answer Questions

What questions do you have about the "space race"? Where can you find the answers to your questions?

"How about a *woman* into space?" Zoe said.

"In those days, people didn't think of women as astronauts," Grandpa explained. "It would take a few dozen years for this country to send women into space.

"But this was the 1950s. There was a feeling of competition in the air. Everyone wanted to know more about 'outer space,' as we called it. Stores filled up with astronaut costumes, model rockets, and small space capsules. We dreamed about flying saucers with flashing lights and little green men from Mars.

competition: challenge

"But if the United States was to be number one," continued Grandpa, "American kids had to be the smartest. Around this time there was a big push for more science in the schools. There were science fairs and science competitions and awards for the best projects. If you were a smart kid like I was, loved science, and were willing to work, all doors were open to you."

Strategy Tool Kit
Make Inferences
What does Grandpa mean when he says, "all doors were open to you"?

CHAPTER 2 Open Doors

"It's getting chilly," said Grandpa, looking at the goose bumps on Zoe's arm. "Why don't you run up and get a jacket? That is, if you want to hear more."

Zoe did. She ran into the house and came back wearing a jacket and carrying a bowl of popcorn. She placed it between them. Grandpa grabbed a handful; Zoe ate hers one at a time.

"You were saying how all doors were open to you," she prompted.

prompted: reminded

"There was a science fair at my school," said Grandpa. "I wanted to show the different ways the moon can look—so I made a model of it. I **attached** the model to a **globe** so that they both moved together. Then, using a desk lamp as the sun, I lit up the surface of the moon as I slowly moved it around Earth. With the light shining on it, the shape of the moon kept changing, just as it does in real life. Here, I'll show you."

Grandpa drew something on a napkin and passed it to Zoe.

"Wow!" said Zoe, astonished that her Grandpa had been only 11. "I bet you won first prize," she said.

"Third," said Grandpa. "But I did win first prize the year after that, with my moon orbit model. It showed how **gravity** keeps the moon in orbit around Earth. Gravity is like a rope that pulls objects in space toward each other."

"Oh yeah, I just reviewed that at school," said Zoe.

"Then you know more than scientists did a few hundred years ago. They thought objects in the sky stayed in place. They thought that the sun, stars, and planets circled around Earth."

"What changed their minds?"

astonished: surprised

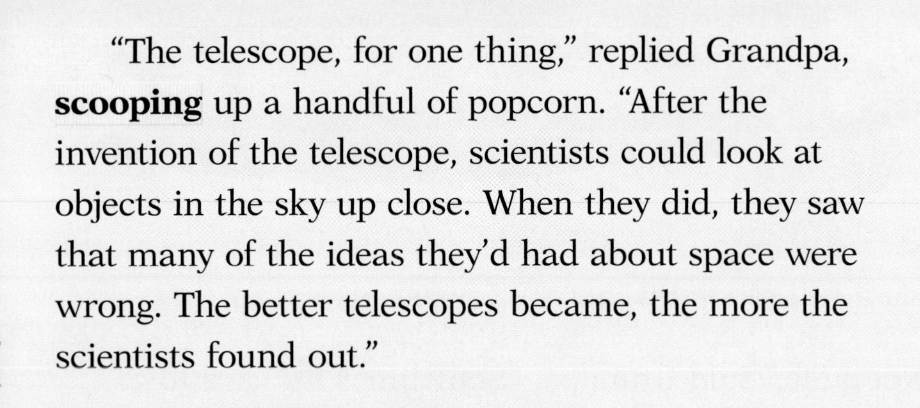

"The telescope, for one thing," replied Grandpa, **scooping** up a handful of popcorn. "After the invention of the telescope, scientists could look at objects in the sky up close. When they did, they saw that many of the ideas they'd had about space were wrong. The better telescopes became, the more the scientists found out."

Stop and Think

This selection tells more than one story. Which story takes place now? Which story takes place in the past?

Faces of the Moon

"Is that a full moon up there?" Zoe asked.

"Not quite," said Grandpa. "Sometimes it's hard to see small differences in the **phases** of the moon."

"You want to hear something funny, Grandpa? When I was younger, I mixed up *phases* of the moon with *faces* of the moon. That's why I always believed there was a man in the moon."

"Instead, there was a man *on* the moon," said Grandpa.

"You could have been him, Grandpa," said Zoe. "That's what I told my friends—that you used to be an astronaut and almost walked on the moon."

Grandpa laughed; it was a real laugh, not a chuckle.

"Yes," he said. "Not many people know that."

"I forget why you didn't get to go," said Zoe. "What happened again?"

“You know very well what happened.”

“But I want you to tell me again,” said Zoe, standing firm.

“Okay,” said Grandpa, “you win. Now where should I start?”

“Start with President Kennedy.”

firm: strong

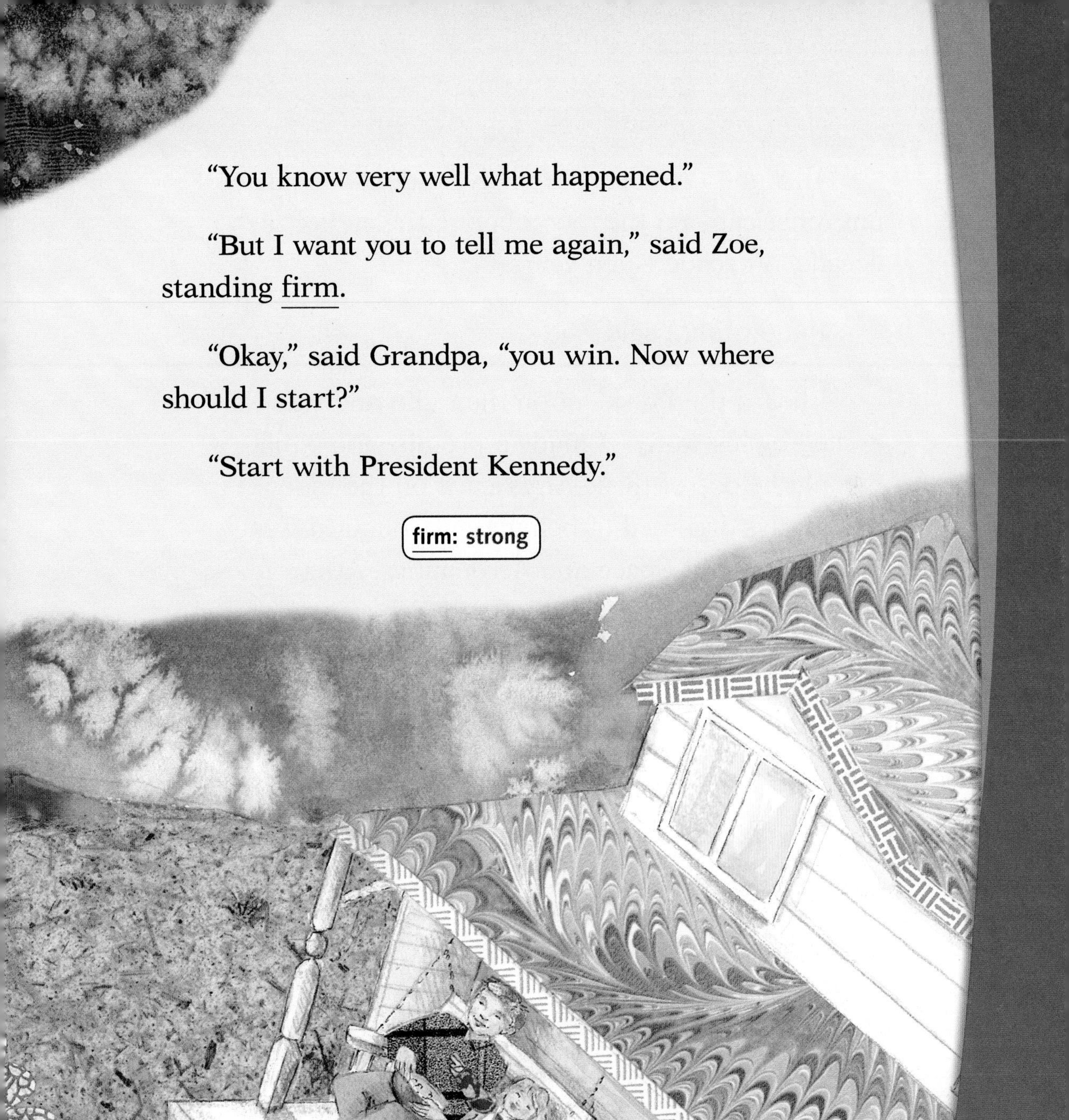

"All right. President Kennedy made a promise to put Americans on the moon before the end of the decade. A decade is ten years."

"I know *that,*" said Zoe.

"I heard the President on the radio and was very excited by his words. I made a promise too—that I would be one of those Americans on the moon. I had always dreamed of being an astronaut. I went to the School of Space and Aeronautics. After graduation, NASA invited me to join their new

Apollo moon mission project. Well, you can just imagine!

"Working on the Apollo project was very exciting. First we sent up some unmanned satellites to take pictures of the moon. Then we sent up satellites that landed on the moon and took pictures of the **lunar** surface.

"That **paved** the way for the first manned orbit around the moon. A year later, in 1969—just as the President had said—two Americans, Neil Armstrong and Buzz Aldrin, took their famous moonwalk. I didn't know them except by name. There are lots of astronauts at NASA."

"After that, there were five more moon landings. The last one, Apollo 17, was in 1972. That's the one I was *supposed* to be on. And would have been, if only I hadn't caught your dad's cold—he was about two then—and the job went to another astronaut.

"As you might guess, astronauts had to be very fit to go into space. Even so, many of them got 'space sick.' Floating around in zero gravity can be very hard on the human body."

"I'll bet," said Zoe.

"Anyway," Grandpa went on, "it wasn't the end of the world. I stayed with NASA and studied the numerous samples of moon rocks the astronauts brought back, hoping to find some signs of life."

"But there were none," Zoe said sadly.

"That's true. There were none. The soil and rock samples I studied held no sign of plant or animal life, past or present."

"So that's that," said Zoe. "But is there life anywhere else in the solar system?"

numerous: many

"Many scientists think so," answered Grandpa. "Right now there are **probes** and other instruments flying through space taking photos. And we have telescopes with lenses eight feet across that can see far into space. We know a lot more than we did when I started out."

"Like what?" Zoe asked.

"Well, there are signs of the possibility of life on the moons around Jupiter. We also have proof that there's a whole other solar system. I'd say we'll know for sure in about five years."

"You know, Grandpa," said Zoe, "by the time I'm a grown-up there won't be anything left to discover."

"How wrong you are!" said Grandpa. "Ideas about space change as we learn more. There will always be things to **marvel** at. As we invent better and better instruments, more pieces of the puzzle snap into place. But there are many, *many* things we still have to explore. I'll leave that to the younger scientists."

Suddenly Grandpa was on his feet. "Let's pay a visit to Professor Mendez at the university," he said.

university: school

"But Grandpa!" cried Zoe, strapping herself into the front seat of Grandpa's car. "It's so late! No one's at the university now!"

"Oh, he's there, all right!" Grandpa said.

When they got to the university, Grandpa parked in a space that said "For Staff Only."

"They mean former staff too," he told Zoe.

They walked through the big glass doors and were met by a security guard.

"Hey, professor!" the guard greeted Grandpa warmly. Grandpa patted him on the back and asked about his family. Then he asked if Professor Mendez was there.

"Elevator to the observatory," said the guard.

former: past

Felix Mendez was glad to see his old professor and to finally meet his granddaughter.

"Zoe here wants to be an astronomer," said Grandpa. "But she's worried that by the time she's grown there won't be anything left to discover."

"Oh, I wouldn't worry about that!" Professor Mendez said. "Did you know that scientists at this university have just discovered another planet?"

Strategy Tool Kit

Ask and Answer Queestions

What is Zoe worried about? Where in the text can you find the answer?

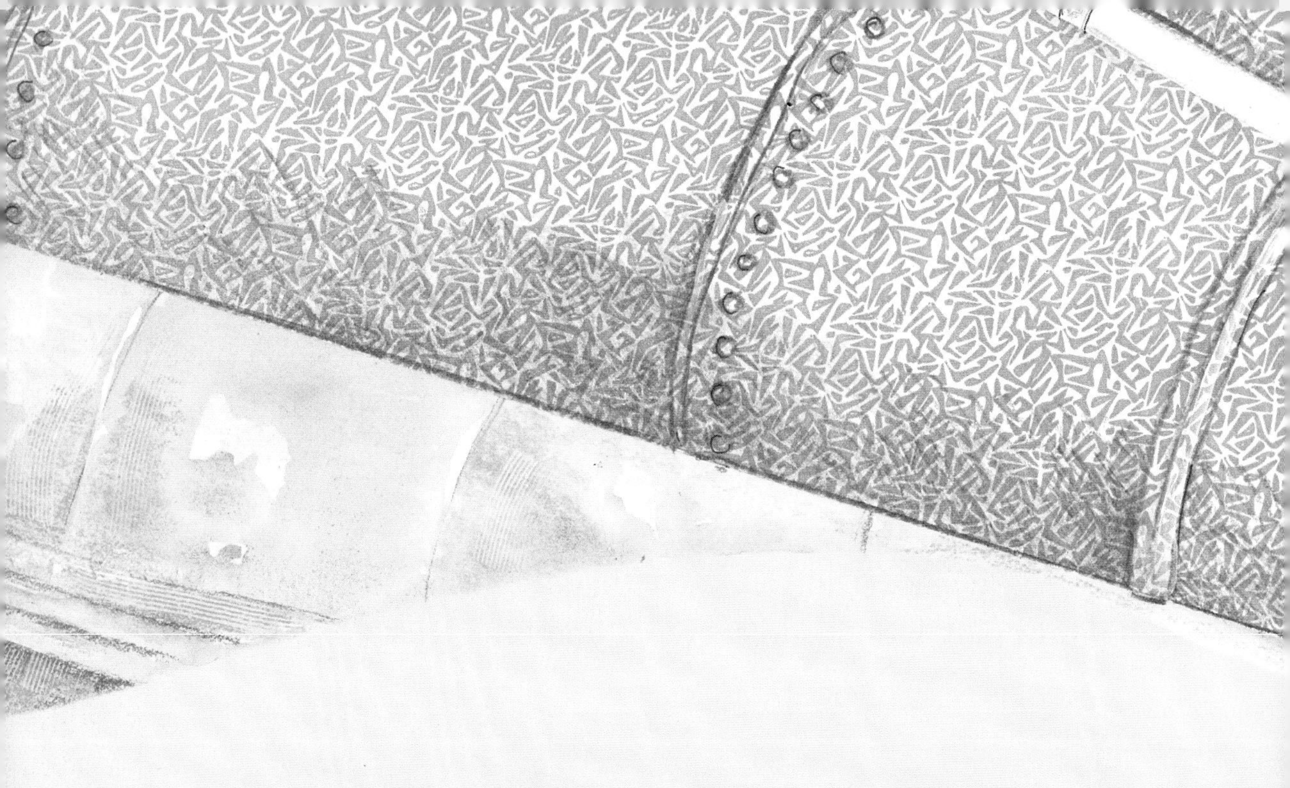

Zoe looked surprised. So did Grandpa.

Professor Mendez continued. “It’s the fifth planet to be discovered around the star 55 Cancri, which makes it at least the 265th planet scientists have discovered since 1995. It’s so far away, we can’t see it even with our most powerful telescopes.”

“Then how do you know it’s there?” asked Zoe.

“We can see a star that’s pretty close,” said Professor Mendez. “It’s very dim, so when an orbiting planet passes in front of it, there’s a little **flicker**; sort of like a mini eclipse. Now *that* we can see,” he added. “In fact, that’s what I was just looking at.

“You see, Zoe,” he continued, “today we’re dealing with planets that are so far away we can’t see them. We can only see how they’ve changed by studying the things around them. It takes a long time to prove a planet’s existence this way—at least 15 years.”

As Zoe looked through the telescope, she thought about the discoveries she hoped to be making in 15 years. She imagined being the first person to discover a planet with life on it. *Maybe,* she thought, *they will call it Planet Zoe.*

Focus Question: How do people view space today?

A Check Understanding

Think about the different tools used for space exploration. How do these tools help us get a better view of space today? PRACTICE COMPANION 339

B Understand Literary Elements

Imagery is language that describes how someone or something looks, sounds, feels, smells, or tastes. Look for examples of imagery in your selection. Share your examples with a partner.

C Share and Compare

Make a list of space exploration tools discussed in your selection. Compare your list with a partner's list. Which tools are the same? Which tools are different? Why?

D Think Critically

Why do people study space? Use examples from the selection to explain.

Think Ahead
Selection 4

Focus Question: How might space be a part of our future?

Selection Connection

In *Spaceman* you learned how people view space today. In the next selection you will learn what inspires people to study space.

Show What You Know

Think about the following: *space stations*; *minerals on other planets*; and *traveling to other planets*. How will these help space be a part of our future? Write your ideas.

PRACTICE COMPANION **340**

Preview

How might space be a part of our future? Preview pages 80–102. Then read *The Opal Mines of Mars* to find out.

Selection 4

The Opal Mines of MARS

by Kathy Zahler

Illustrated by Nathan Hale

Cast of Characters

JASON: a 24-year-old miner

DIZ: his boss

ACT 1 SCENE 1: An office on Mars

(It is early morning in an empty high-tech office. JASON, *a miner dressed in astronaut gear, sits in front of a computer screen. Light shines from the screen.)*

JASON: *(Talking at screen.)* Cliff? Hey, Cliff! How's it going? Yes, I made it, I'm here! What a trip! *(He listens.)* Well, it is interesting. They took us underground yesterday for the first time. My gear is pretty heavy . . .
No, I can't wait to get started!

*(*Diz *enters. Like* Jason, *she is dressed in astronaut gear. She carries her helmet.)*

Jason: *(Looks at the screen.)* Sure, I'll be careful. It's just like mining on Earth, so far. Remember, though, one Mars opal is worth more than 100 Earth **diamonds**!

*(*Diz *points to a clock on the wall.)*

Jason: *(Looks at the clock.)* Hey, Cliff. I have to go. I will call again next month. *(He turns off the screen and follows* Diz *out of the office.)*

opal: shiny stone

Strategy Tool Kit

Ask and Answer Questions

What questions do you have about where Jason is? Where can you find the answers?

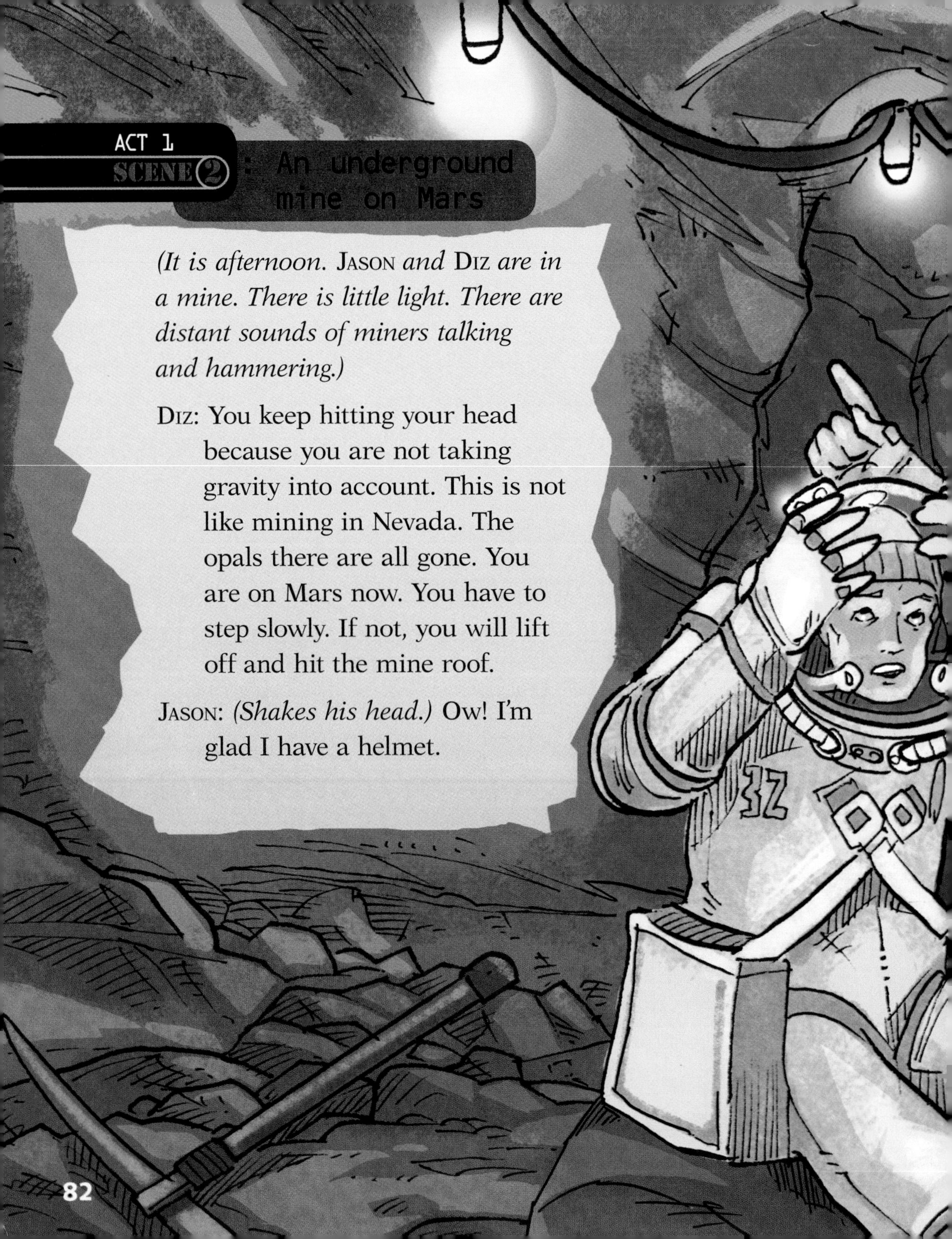

ACT 1 SCENE 2: An underground mine on Mars

(It is afternoon. JASON *and* DIZ *are in a mine. There is little light. There are distant sounds of miners talking and hammering.)*

DIZ: You keep hitting your head because you are not taking gravity into account. This is not like mining in Nevada. The opals there are all gone. You are on Mars now. You have to step slowly. If not, you will lift off and hit the mine roof.

JASON: *(Shakes his head.)* Ow! I'm glad I have a helmet.

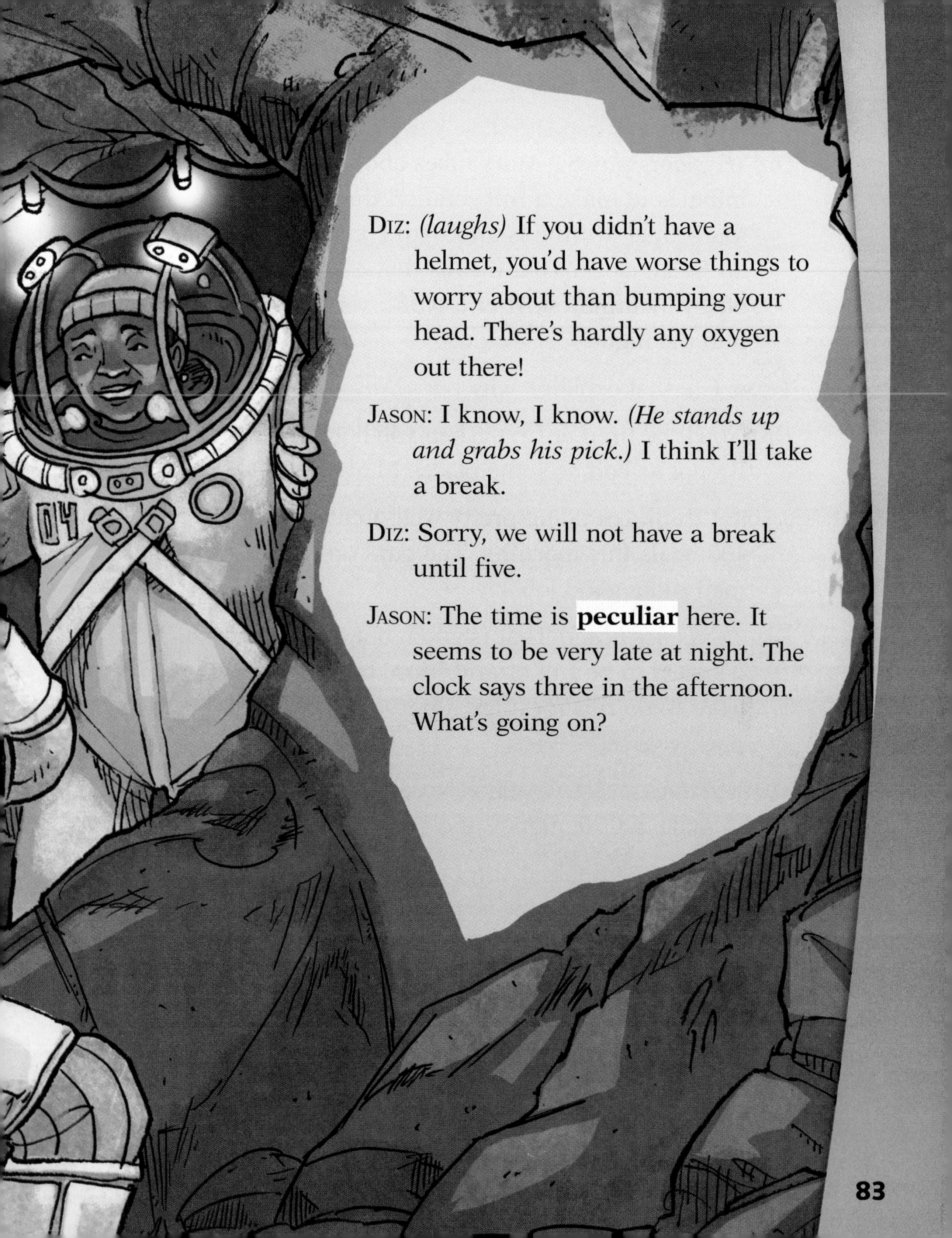

Diz: *(laughs)* If you didn't have a helmet, you'd have worse things to worry about than bumping your head. There's hardly any oxygen out there!

Jason: I know, I know. *(He stands up and grabs his pick.)* I think I'll take a break.

Diz: Sorry, we will not have a break until five.

Jason: The time is **peculiar** here. It seems to be very late at night. The clock says three in the afternoon. What's going on?

DIZ: *(Explains slowly.)* Mars takes about 39 more minutes to make a full rotation than Earth does. Mars Opal Mining is an Earth company. We use an Earth clock. That means that every day we're off by 39 minutes. After a while, we're working into the night.

JASON: Oh, that explains why I'm always tired.

DIZ: You'll be tired at first. Then you'll get used to it. It's not as bad as some places I have been!

JASON: I think I'm doing pretty well. I cut out about 100 opals this morning. The guys on the line told me I did a good job.

DIZ: *(Nods her head.)* That is good, but don't overdo it. It's good to be full of **ambition**, but if you want to do this for a few years, you'll need to **pace** yourself.

JASON: *(Laughs.)* A few years? No, I just need this job to make a little money and then go home.

DIZ: It's not just a job; it can be a career. Look at me. I've been in space for nearly 20 years and I'm nowhere near ready to leave.

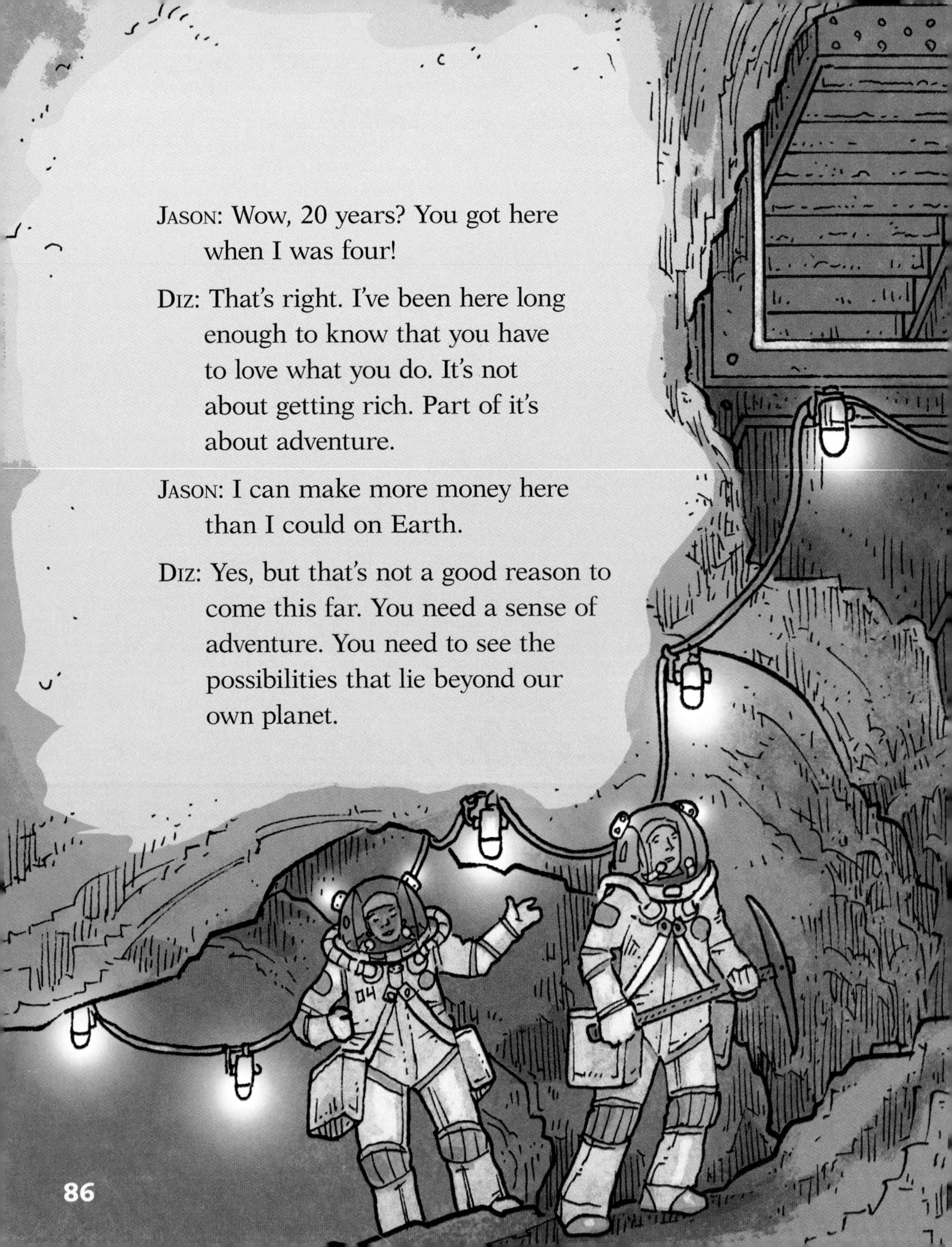

JASON: Wow, 20 years? You got here when I was four!

DIZ: That's right. I've been here long enough to know that you have to love what you do. It's not about getting rich. Part of it's about adventure.

JASON: I can make more money here than I could on Earth.

DIZ: Yes, but that's not a good reason to come this far. You need a sense of adventure. You need to see the possibilities that lie beyond our own planet.

JASON: I'm not sure what you mean.

DIZ: Well, we are among the first to mine here on Mars. It's exciting to be the first, don't you think? We live in a clean, modern mining camp inside a bubble. We're the first ones to do that!

JASON: I guess so. I don't plan to stay in space for 20 years, though. *(He exits.)*

DIZ: *(cheerfully)* I didn't plan to, either. Sometimes things just happen!

Strategy Tool Kit
Visualize
Based on Diz's description, what do you think the mining camp looks like?

ACT 2

SCENE 1: An office on Mars

(A month has passed. It is daytime. JASON *is in a bright, high-tech office. His friend's face is on a screen.)*

JASON: Hey, Cliff? Yes, I can hear you . . . Wow! I haven't been hiking in a long time. That sounds great. No, there's not much to do here. Today's my day off. I can't even go for a walk, really. My gear belongs to the mining company. I can only wear it in the mine. *(He listens.)*

Yes, I've found a lot of opals. We all have. We have to account for every one of them. They all go back to Earth. The company sells them. No, I'm not getting rich. Not really. I make a good **salary**. That's about it.

DIZ: *(Enters in a hurry.)* Jason, we need you. There's a problem at the mine.

JASON: *(Looks at the screen.)* Cliff, I have to go! I'll talk to you next month.

Stop and Think

How do you think Jason feels about being on Mars?

ACT 2 SCENE 2: An underground mine on Mars

(It is a few minutes later, deep in the mine. Jason *and* Diz *and other miners each ride in an open car. The cars form a train. The lights they hold cast shadows on the shiny walls. A dripping sound can be heard.)*

Jason: Wow, we're pretty deep in the mine!

Diz: This is just about as far down as we get.

Jason: Are the opals bigger down here?

Diz: Not really. But the company wants to make sure we find every opal there is to find. That's why we all keep digging, even though we don't really like to dig this far.

JASON: Is this where the missing miners are supposed to be?

DIZ: They called from down on this level. Be quiet now. Try to hear them. *(She exits the train car.* JASON *follows her.* DIZ *taps on the wall of the mine. She walks along, tapping.)*

JASON: Do you hear anything?

DIZ: Shh. *(She continues to walk and tap.* JASON *follows. At times he presses his ear to the wall.)*

JASON: Is that dripping water I hear?

DIZ: It may be. Without water we'd have no opals. The water picks up the mineral silica as it runs through cracks in the rock. Once the water evaporates, opals form.

JASON: What's that tapping? *(They both stand still.)*

DIZ: You have good ears! I hear it too. *(She taps a button on her handset, and a communications image appears in front of her.)* We're in the lower level, about half a click in. There's been a rock slide. Yes, send the machine. Let me know when everyone is found. *(The screen disappears.)* The machine will come and quickly dig them out.

JASON: *(surprised)* That's it? What do we do now?

DIZ: We can head back out. The machine will do the work. I am sure the miners will be fine. This happens every few weeks. You shouldn't be surprised. There were cave-ins at the mines in Nevada too.

JASON: I know. I guess danger is part of the adventure.

(He shivers, but he follows DIZ *back into the train car, which rolls to exit.)*

click: kilometer

Strategy Tool Kit

Ask and Answer Questions

What questions would you have about the information on these pages? Find the answers in the text or another source.

ACT 3 SCENE 1: An office on Mars

(A month has passed. JASON *is alone in the high-tech office. He is looking at a bright computer screen.)*

JASON: No, Cliff. I'm starting to think I made a **rash** decision. I do not know how Diz stands it. You know, Diz, my boss. She has been in space for 20 years! She likes the adventure of it! Can you believe that? *(He listens.)* No, there is no real way to get rich. The company gets rich, but the workers don't. *(He listens.)* Well, how are things on Earth? Are there jobs? No? That's right. I'm thinking about coming back.

(He listens.) Really? Things are that bad? Well, I don't know. I can't make a career of this. Diz keeps saying it will get better. She tells me to think of it as a grand adventure. I feel as though the adventure part has not really started yet!

*(*DIZ *enters with boxes. She starts to pack up some things from the office.* JASON *does not see her.)*

JASON: *(Looks at the computer.)* Well, I should go. I'll let you know what I decide. *(He shuts off the computer. For a minute he holds his head in his hands.)*

DIZ: Is everything all right?

JASON: *(Jumps a little.)* Oh! I didn't see you! Umm, yes. I guess everything's okay. *(*DIZ *continues to pack.)* What are you doing?

DIZ: Packing up.

JASON: I can see that. Why are you packing up?

DIZ: I have a new job.

JASON: A new job? Where? Are they opening a new mine?

DIZ: Yes. *(She keeps packing.* JASON *waits.* DIZ *stops packing and sits down next to him.)* A new mine . . . on Phobos.

JASON: Phobos??? Wow! They're sending you to one of Mars's moons?

DIZ: *(proudly)* Well, I know how to set things up. I know how to be the first. I'm the right person to send. I was one of the first to test the rings of Saturn. I was one of the first to mine on Mars. I like being the first.

JASON: Wow, Phobos. *(He pauses.)* It's a great adventure! You have a chance that few people have. You can make a great mining camp on Phobos! *(He thinks for a minute.)* Will you take other miners with you?

DIZ: We'll start with a small **staff**. We don't yet know what we might find on Phobos. It may be one of the oldest bodies in the solar system. Who knows what we might find buried there?

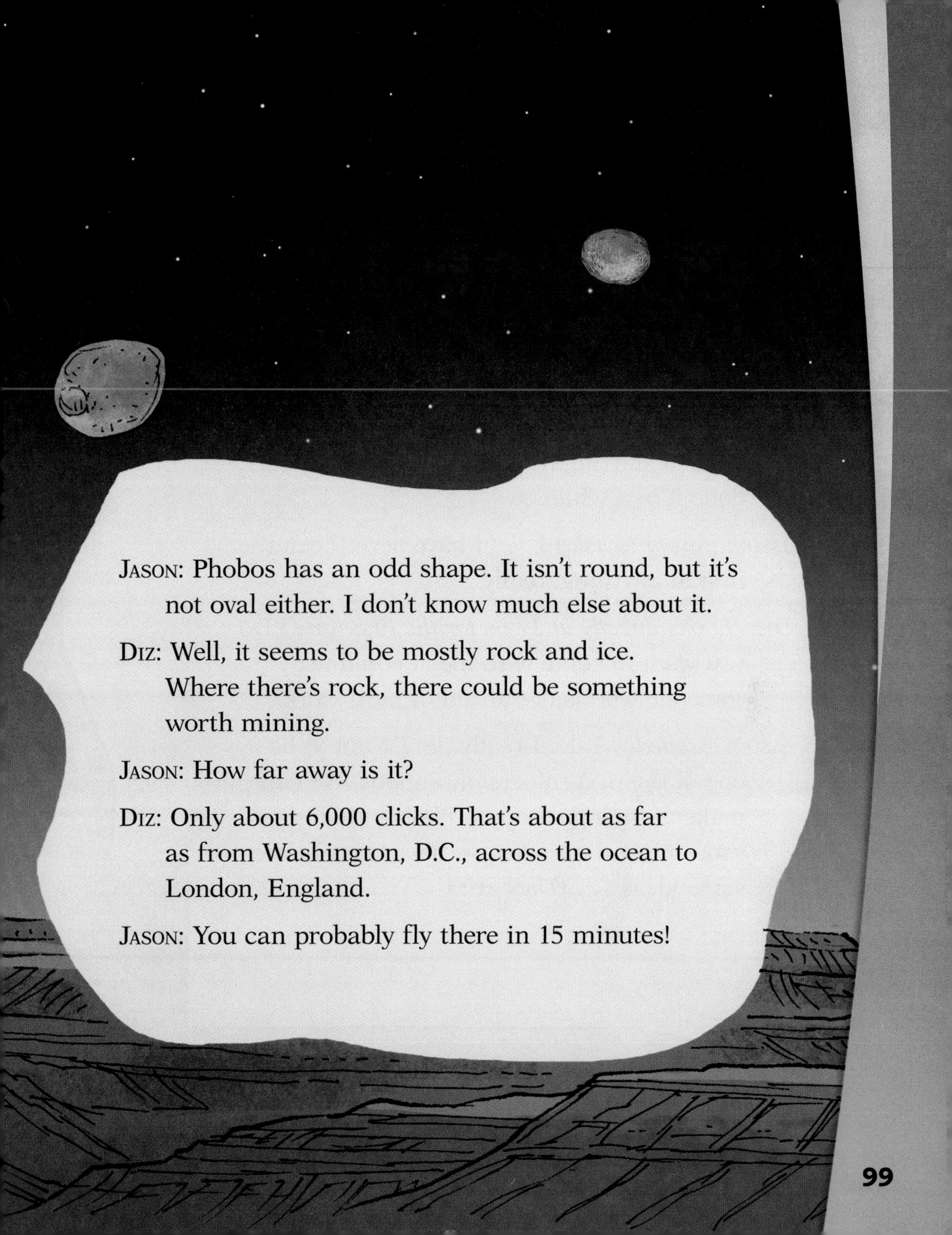

JASON: Phobos has an odd shape. It isn't round, but it's not oval either. I don't know much else about it.

DIZ: Well, it seems to be mostly rock and ice. Where there's rock, there could be something worth mining.

JASON: How far away is it?

DIZ: Only about 6,000 clicks. That's about as far as from Washington, D.C., across the ocean to London, England.

JASON: You can probably fly there in 15 minutes!

DIZ: Yes, you're right. It's a short trip. We'll start some kind of lunar bus to take us back and forth from Mars to Phobos. That way, if we find something there, we can bring over as many miners as we need.

JASON: Will you really be the first one to set foot on Phobos?

DIZ: That's right. It's a new step in my career. I'm good at starting new things. I just haven't done it in a while.

JASON: *(Afraid to ask.)* I . . . I have never been the first at anything, really.

DIZ: *(Looks directly at* JASON *for the first time.)* Do you want to come with me? I could use someone who is not afraid of hard work.

JASON: *(excitedly)* I do. I really do. I want to be one of the first miners on Phobos. We can make a mining camp on Phobos that is ten times nicer than what we have here. I have some ideas . . . *(They exit.)*

Strategy Tool Kit
Make Connections
What is something you have been excited to be a part of?

ACT 3 SCENE 2: An office on Mars

(It is a few days later. Jason *is back in the office. The light from the computer screen shines on* Jason.*)*

Jason: That's right, Cliff. Diz and I are going to lead the team. Well, she will head up the team, but I will help. We're going to land on Phobos. No one has ever landed there before. It's a real adventure. We'll set up a lunar camp. It might end up being the best mining camp in the solar system. Of course, we don't know what we'll find on Phobos. That's what makes it interesting! It's not about getting rich. It's about the adventure! There is so much **potential** beyond Earth. I can't wait to get started!

Focus Question: How might space be a part of our future?

A Check Understanding

Using ideas from the selection, make a list of the ways space may be a part of our future. Do you think these events will happen? PRACTICE COMPANION 359

B Understand Literary Elements

A motive is the reason why a character does something. Motives tell you what a character wants. How do Jason's motives for being a miner change? What does this tell you about his character? Discuss your answers with a partner.

C Share and Compare

With a partner, compare your list of the ways space may be a part of our future. How does your partner's list differ from yours? How is it the same?

D Think Critically

Why do people study space? Use examples from the selection to explain.

Respond to the THEME Question

Why do people study space?

Use these activities to show what you've learned about the theme question.

Design and Create

1. Imagine that you discovered a new constellation. Design your own model of it.
2. Draw your constellation on black construction paper. Cut out small holes for stars to form the shape of the constellation.
3. Shine a light behind the paper to see the shape that the stars would make in the sky.

Multimedia

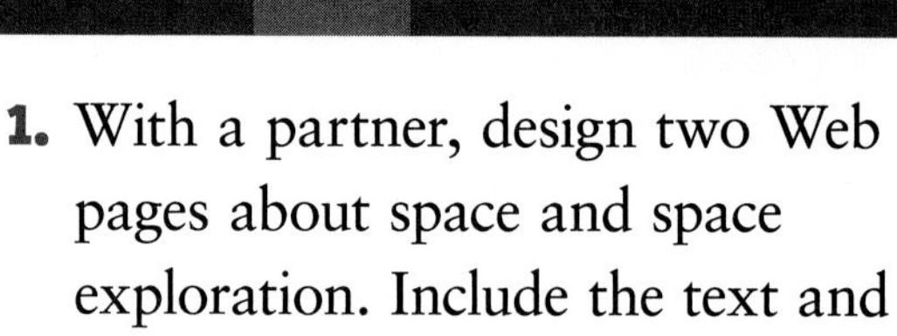

1. With a partner, design two Web pages about space and space exploration. Include the text and pictures that you want on your Web pages.

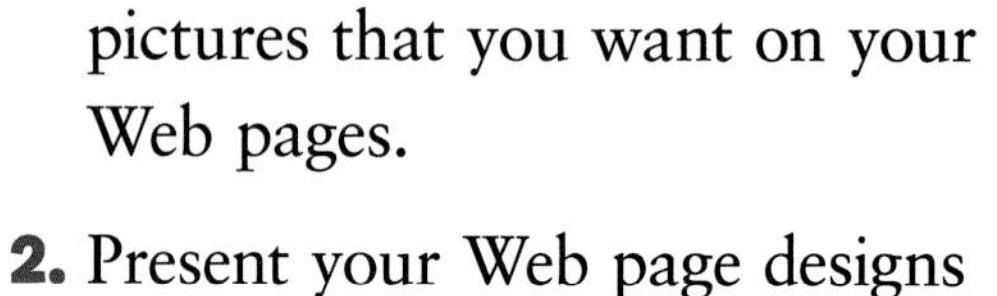

2. Present your Web page designs to the class.

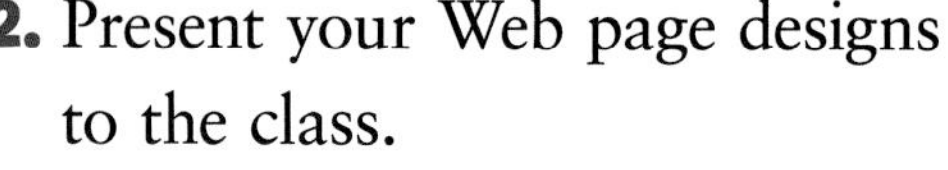

1. Choose your favorite selection from the unit. Tell your group why you chose it.
2. Read your favorite part aloud.
3. Search for other books about space to read and share.

1. Imagine that your town is located on the moon.
2. Write a story that describes your daily life. Think about how life on the moon is different from the life you live on Earth. Be sure to include dialogue between characters.
3. Read your story to a friend.

Glossary

Pronunciation Key

a	bat	oi	toy
ā	ape	ou	sh**ou**t
air	**air**	ŏŏ	b**oo**k
ä	p**a**rk	ōō	m**oo**n
e	l**e**t	s	**s**un
ē	**e**asy	sh	pre**ss**ure
i	**i**f	th	**th**e, **th**ing
ī	l**ie**	u	n**u**t
îr	d**ear**	ûr	c**ir**cle
k	**c**ause	ə	**a**go
o	l**o**t	ər	moth**er**
ō	g**o**	′	primary stress
ô	**a**ll	′	secondary stress

ambition (am bish′ ən) *n.* a desire for a goal;
My ambition is to open my own restaurant someday. **84**

attach (ə tach′) *v.* to fasten;
I attach clothes pins to the clothes so they can dry on the line. **63**

classify (klas′ ə fī′) *v.* to arrange, organize, or categorize;
Vijay likes to classify the rocks in his collection according to color. **13**

conquer (kong′ kər) *v.* to gain mastery over something;
To climb the tree I need to conquer my fear of heights. **58**

depart (di pärt′) *v.* to go away;
When does the train depart for Charleston? **34**

desire (di zīr′) *v.* to hope for or want something;
Some people desire an exciting vacation, while others enjoy staying home. **19**

diamond (dī′ mənd) *n.* a mineral made of pure carbon in the form of a clear crystal;
A diamond is a very valuable gem. **81**

emerge (i mûrj′) *v.* to come into view;
Soon the moon will emerge from behind those clouds. **35**

flare (flair) *n.* a sudden, glaring light;
We saw a flare in the distance from the brush fire. **44**

flicker (flik′ ər) *n.* a quick, unsteady light;
We saw the flicker of the candle's flame in the breeze. **76**

formation (fôr mā′ shən) *n.* something that is made, arranged, or formed, as in a pattern;
The formation of rocks looked like an archway. **58**

galaxy (gal′ ək sē) *n.* very large groups of stars and other matter found throughout the universe;
Our solar system is part of the Milky Way galaxy. **9**

globe (glōb) *n.* a representation of Earth, the moon, or an other planet, in the shape of a sphere;
We have a very large globe in our classroom that we use to find different countries. **63**

gravity (gra′ vi tē) *n.* the force that pulls things toward Earth;
Gravity holds us down and keeps everything from floating up into space. **64**

irregular (i reg′ yə lər) *adj.* uneven or not following a pattern;
This skirt has an irregular edge. **14**

lunar (lōō′ nər) *adj.* having to do with the moon;
A lunar landing vehicle transported the astronauts across the moon's surface. **69**

magnetic (mag net′ ik) *adj.* relating to magnets or the pull of magnetism;
A magnetic calendar will stick to most metal surfaces. **44**

magnificent (mag ni′ fə sənt) *adj.* very grand and beautiful;
We saw a magnificent sunrise over the mountains. **58**

marvel (mär′ vəl) *v.* to feel a sense of wonder or astonishment;
My friends marvel at how long I can do my handstands. **73**

nebulae (neb′ yə lē′) *n.* clouds of gas or dust in outer space;
On some nights we can see nebulae in the night sky. **9**

pace (pās) *v.* to walk or proceed at a slow or measured rate;
Greg knows how to pace himself during a marathon so he doesn't get tired too quickly. **84**

pave (pāv) *v.* to prepare the way or make something easier;
My older brothers' experiences will help pave the way for me in high school. **69**

peculiar (pi kyōōl′ yər) *adj.* odd or strange;
Hot pink is a peculiar color for a bus. **83**

phase (fāz) *n.* the appearance or state of the moon or a planet;
This Saturday night we'll see the moon's full phase. **66**

portray (pôr trā′) *v.* to describe or show in pictures or words;
The murals portray the history of our town. **33**

potential (pə ten′ shəl) *n.* something that can become actual;
The radar map shows that there is a potential for thunderstorms to develop. **102**

prism (priz′ əm) *n.* a transparent, usually glass, form that separates a beam of light into colors;
Mom has a prism in the window that makes a rainbow on the kitchen wall. **42**

probe (prōb) *n.* a device that is used to obtain and send back information from space;
NASA might send up a space probe to get information about the different planets' atmospheres. **72**

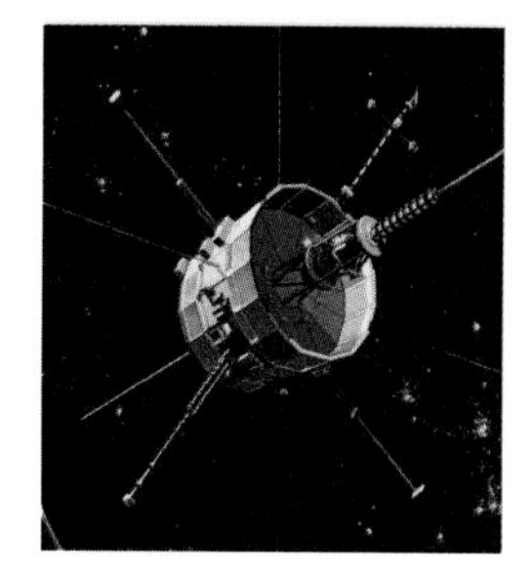

project (prə jekt′) *v.* to cause light, a shadow, or an image to fall onto a surface;
The flashlight will project its light into the dark room. **40**

pulse (puls) *v.* to beat or throb;
I can feel my blood pulse if I touch my wrist in a certain place. **48**

puzzle (puz′ əl) *n.* a question or problem;
It was a puzzle as to how the goldfish got out of the fish tank. **15**

rash (rash) *adj.* hasty or done without thought;
We made a rash choice when we decided to ride our bikes even though the forecast was for thunderstorms. **94**

reflect (ri flekt′) *v.* to give back, bounce off;
That mirror will reflect the sun's light very strongly. **7**

revolve (ri volv′) *v.* to move in a circle around a center point;
The desserts revolve in the restaurant's display case. **12**

rotate (rō′ tāt) *v.* to turn on an axis;
Planets rotate on their axes as they orbit the sun. **12**

salary (sal′ rē) *n.* a fixed amount of money paid regularly for work done;
Lisa will be paid a salary for walking Mr. Kotter's dogs every day. **88**

scoop (skōōp) *v.* to pick up quickly with a sweep of the hand;
I will scoop up some snow and make a big snowball. **65**

sparkle (spär′ kəl) *v.* to shine in quick, bright flashes;
I love the way the stars sparkle on a clear, dark night. **6**

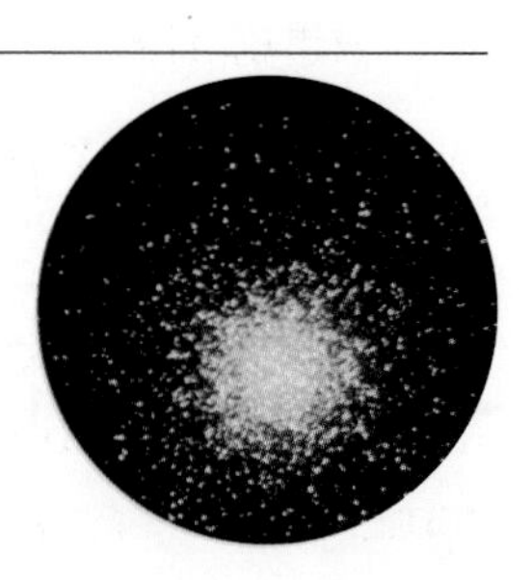

staff (staf) *n.* the group of workers who help carry out a task;
The staff in the school office help the school run smoothly. **98**

telescope (te′ lə skōp′) *n.* an instrument that makes faraway objects seem larger and closer;
Mom's telescope is very powerful, so we can see some planets. **6**

universe (yōō′ nə vûrs′) *n.* everything that exists, including Earth, the planets, and everything in space;
The entire universe is larger than you can imagine. **16**

visible (viz′ ə bəl) *adj.* able to be seen;
Emma's apartment is visible from the street. **42**

Index

Acknowledgments

Photo Credits: Cover ©Royalty-Free/Corbis; **4** ©Photodisc/Getty Images; **5** (tl) ©Alamy Images, (tr) ©Leda_d/Shutterstock, (bl) ©Comstock Images/Alamy, (br) ©NASA; **6** ©Royalty-Free/Corbis; **6–27** (border) ©BrandXPictures/Punchstock; **7** (t) ©The McGraw-Hill Companies, Inc., (b) ©Bettmann/Corbis; **8** ©Yerkes Observatory Photography; **9** ©NASA; **10** ©Roger Ressmeyer/Corbis; **11** ©NASA; **12** ©NASA; **13** ©The Huntington Library; **14** ©Aura Gemini Observatory; **15** (l) ©Bettmann/Corbis, (r) ©NASA; **16** ©Emilio Segré Visual Archives/American Institute of Physics/Photo Researchers, Inc.; **17** ©Bettmann/Corbis; **18** ©PhotoDisc/Getty Images; **19** ©Margaret Bourke-White/Time & Life Pictures/Getty Images; **20–21** ©Roger Ressmeyer/Corbis; **22** ©Associated Press; **23** ©Roger Ressmeyer/Corbis; **24** ©The CalTech Archives; **25** ©J.R. Eyerman/Time & Life Pictures/Getty Images; **26** ©Photodisc/Getty Images; **27** ©USPS; **28** ©StockTrek/AGE Fotostock; **29** (l) ©Leda_d/Shutterstock, (r) ©Alamy Images; **30–31** ©Royalty-Free/Corbis; **32, 34, 36,** (border) ©Royalty-Free/Corbis; **32** ©Christine Osborne/Corbis; **33** ©The Granger Collection, New York; **36** ©DAJ/Alamy Images; **37** ©Johnathan Blair/Corbis; **38, 40, 42, 44** (border) ©DAJ/Alamy Images; **38** ©Bettmann/Corbis; **39** (t) ©Photodisc/Getty Images, (b) ©Gary Hincks/Photo Researchers, Inc.; **40** ©Library of Congress; **41** ©Digital Vision/Punchstok; **42** ©Photodisc/Getty Images; **43** ©NASA; **44** ©U.S. Naval Research Laboratory; **45** ©Andrew Holt/Photographer's Choice/Getty Images; **46–47** ©Steve A. Musinger/Photo Researchers, Inc.; **48** ©NASA; **48–49** ©Photodisc/Getty Images; **50, 52** (border) ©Photodisc/Getty Images; **51** ©NASA; **52–53** ©Digital Stock/Corbis; **54** ©U.S. Naval Research Laboratory; **55** (t) ©NASA, (b) ©Comstock Images/Alamy; **79** (t) ©Brand X Pictures/PunchStock, (b) ©Pixtal/Agefotostock.

Art Credits: 34–35 ©The McGraw-Hill Companies, Inc./Gwenda Kaczor; **56–78** ©The McGraw-Hill Companies, Inc./Janice Fried; **80–103** ©The McGraw-Hill Companies, Inc./Nathan Hale.